London
in a Lunchtime

howtobooks

Please send for a free copy of the latest catalogue to:
How To Books, 3 Newtec Place, Magdalen Road, Oxford OX4 1RE United Kingdom
email: info@howtobooks.co.uk
http://www.howtobooks.co.uk

London
in a Lunchtime
...or whenever you've an hour to spare

howtobooks

ANN HALL & LUCHO PAYNE

Published by How To Books Ltd,
3 Newtec Place, Magdalen Road,
Oxford OX4 1RE. United Kingdom.
Tel: (01865) 793806. Fax: (01865) 248780
email: info@howtobooks.co.uk
http://www.howtobooks.co.uk

First published 2002

British Library Cataloguing in Publication Data.
A catalogue record for this book is available from the British Library.

Maps by Nicki Averill
Cover design by Baseline Arts Ltd, Oxford
Cover image, *London – The Thames*, by Christopher Rogers
email: Imagesoflondon@aol.com
Tel/fax: 020 7794 5684
The image of Dr Johnson on page 46 is reproduced by kind permission of Dr Johnson's House Trust

Produced for How To Books by Deer Park Productions
Typeset and design by Baseline Arts Ltd, Oxford
Printed and bound in Great Britain by Bell & Bain Ltd., Glasgow

Contents

Contents

We've tried to ensure that all information is correct, but if you find any details regarding opening times, admission charges etc. differ from those stated in the book, please let us know. You'll find our email address on the second page of this book. We suggest that you always ring ahead to check that the site you'd like to visit is open.

Preface

The idea for the book first started when we were working in an office near London Bridge Station. One of our colleagues had found out a few interesting snippets of information about the history of the local area and this prompted a few of us to investigate further. We were amazed to discover many fascinating places very close to the office. There was a 16th Century coaching inn frequented by Shakespeare, the remains of Marshalsea Prison which once held Charles Dickens' father and an area known as Bankside which was a notorious adult playground in Elizabethan times packed with brothels and bear-baiting pits.

Having so much history and culture right under our noses led us to think that perhaps, instead of just sitting at our desks eating sandwiches at lunchtime, we could get out of the office and visit a few places. So, an email was sent round the office announcing a lunchtime visit to the Clink Prison Museum – this aroused quite a bit of interest and seven or eight of us spent a very enjoyable lunchtime at the museum. We found out all the sordid and shocking details of the area's history, had a swift half at a nearby pub and returned to the office buzzing with excitement and agreeing that we ought to do something like that again.

A few weeks later, we repeated the process – this time we went to The Old Operating Theatre. Email was again used to organise everyone and once again, the trip was hugely enjoyable. By now our lunchtime 'Culture Club' had been well and truly established – more and more outings were to follow.

At the time we tried to find a book that would help us organise our trips but we were unable to find anything that suited our needs.

So, this prompted us to keep notes of our visits with a view towards creating our own book – to enable others to follow in our footsteps.

So, here's the end result – *London In A Lunchtime* – the book that we were hoping to buy. This book is not just aimed at office workers, like ourselves, it's also aimed at anyone who finds themselves in Central London with an hour or two to spare.

Don't just sit at your desk or hide away in your hotel room – make the most of your time! Use *London In A Lunchtime* as your guide and you'll be amazed at how much you can see and do!

Ann Hall and Lucho Payne

Useful Tips

Here are a few tips and hints that you might find useful:

◆ Always phone first – some sites can close at short notice for special occasions, maintenance, refurbishment etc.

◆ Start with the free sites – to get you in the mood.

◆ If a group of you are going, you may qualify for a group discount on the entry price.

◆ A taxi journey may be the fastest mode of transport at lunchtime and if several of you are going, it's quite cheap when you share.

◆ If you are an office worker and a bit concerned about doing so much on your lunchtime, then do what we did – agree it with you boss and take a couple of shorter lunches during the week of your planned outing. Don't forget to emphasise the team-building aspect – our office became a much livelier and friendlier place and, as a result, productivity increased. You could always invite the boss along as well!

◆ Also, if you're an office worker, you could save some of the longer visits for special occasions such as the completion of a project.

◆ Avoid the really well known sites during the peak tourist season – out of season it's usually possible to walk straight into even the most popular sites. Westminster Abbey and the London Dungeon are good examples of this.

◆ Talk to the staff at the sites – ask them questions. Many of them have a really in-depth knowledge and are very keen to share it when someone shows an interest.

◆ A lot of the pubs that we mention have fascinating histories and stories associated with them. Quite often the details can be found on wall plaques – have a good look round while you're quenching your thirst. If you notice anything unusual or interesting, ask about it behind the bar – its surprising what you can learn!

Date: **Mon, 19 October**
To: **The Culture Club**
From: **Lucho**
Subject: **The London Dungeon**

Continuing with our hugely popular visits to local attractions The Culture Club proudly presents a trip to

..............here follow the gory details............

Date: Friday October 23rd

Time: Leave office 12.00pm

Cost: Adults £8.95 (group rates apply for groups of 20 or more)

Meet the Beast of Whitechapel and Katarina the Vampire Girl !!

Afterwards: Drinks at a local hostelry !!!

..............what to do next............

♦ please send me a reply if you're interested so that we can get an idea of numbers.
♦ also, the Culture Club has a kitty of £20 - this will be used to reduce the admission cost if our group is less than 20.
♦ remember, the more the merrier!

Yours until judgement day,
Lucho

PS. don't forget that in order to take an extended lunch break you'll need to check with your team leader / manager / boss, to make up the time in the week etc.

The Sites

APSLEY HOUSE
Wellington Museum

Apsley House, The Wellington Museum

NO. 1 LONDON!

Hyde Park Corner, London, W1J 7NT
Telephone: 020 7499 5676
Underground: Hyde Park Corner, Green Park
Admission: £4.50 Concessions: £3.00 Over 60s & under 18s: free
A sound guide is included in the price
Length of time required for visit: 1 hour
Open: 11:00 – 17:00 Tue – Sun
Web site: www.apsleyhouse.org.uk

Directions
From Hyde Park
Corner tube
station, take Exit
1 and follow the
signposts. From
Green Park
station, take the
Piccadilly North
Side exit and turn
right at street
level – you'll see
signposts as you
progress along
Piccadilly.

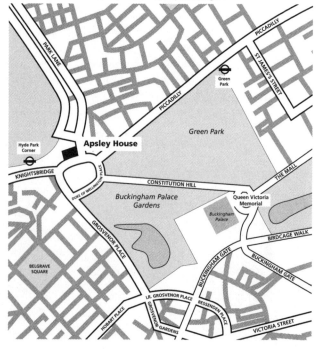

London 1817 – imagine that you've recently had outstanding military successes in India and Denmark, you've liberated Portugal in the Peninsular War and commanded the British, Dutch and German forces at Waterloo where you inflicted the final defeat on Napoleon. You've just been made the 1st Duke of Wellington and have become one of the most honoured men in Europe and possibly the greatest military commander the country has ever known. . .

Now you need somewhere to live – so how does 'No. 1 London' sound? Perfect. Yes, Apsley House was purchased by the 1st Duke of Wellington in 1817 and was known as No. 1 due to its proximity to the toll-gate into London when approaching from the West. A high profile address – quite fitting for the Iron Duke.

Successive Dukes of Wellington lived in Apsley House until 1947 when the House and the collection were presented to the nation by the 7th Duke. Since then the house has been open to the public as the Wellington Museum.

The house today is largely as it was when the 1st Duke lived there. The centre-piece of the house is, without doubt, the stunning Waterloo Gallery. This room, 90 feet long, was added to the house as a setting for the Duke's paintings and as a suitable place for entertaining in style – notably at his annual Waterloo Banquets.

Things weren't all rosy though. The Iron Duke became Prime Minister in 1828 and made some people so unhappy that Apsley House was besieged by an angry mob in 1831.

And how did he look at the end of it all? See for yourself – his death mask can be found in the basement gallery.

And afterwards. . . Take a walk down Piccadilly to the Rose and Crown in Old Park Lane (first left past the Hard Rock Café). Once used as a place to hold prisoners on their way to Tyburn Gallows, this pub has an unusual history – all explained at the front of the pub.

The Bank of England

THE OLD LADY OF THREADNEEDLE STREET – SHE'S FREE!

Barthomolew Lane, London EC2R 8AH
Telephone: 020 7601 4878
Underground: Bank
Admission: FREE
Length of time required for visit: 45 – 50 mins
Open: 10:00am – 5:00pm Monday - Friday
Web site: www.bankofengland.co.uk/museum

Directions
From Bank underground station, take exit 2 (signposted to the Bank Of England). Turn left into Threadneedle Street and walk past the front of the Bank of England – until you reach Bartholomew Lane. Turn left into Bartholomew Lane – the Museum entrance is about 20 yards on the left.

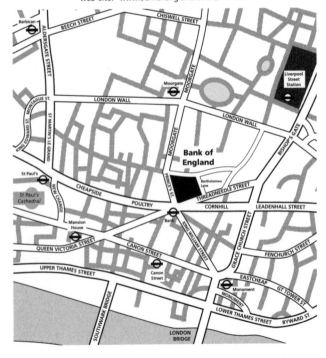

June 7th 1780. The Gordon Riots are in full swing. The rioters have been creating havoc for five days and, amongst other things, have already burned down several prisons (including the notorious Newgate Prison) and released the prisoners. Now they decide to storm the Bank of England. . . but they've left it too late. A militia has been hurriedly raised to guard the bank and has arrived just in time to quell the riots. If the rioters had got there a bit sooner, the bank and its gold bullion would have been at their mercy.

Not much chance of an angry mob storming the bank nowadays but you can find out all about the history of money and the development of the Bank of England, for free, at the Bank of England Museum.

This museum is perfect for a lunchtime visit. You'll be greeted at the door by chaps in pink overcoats and top hats and you can have an audio tour (with audio wand) for just £1.

You can see how the Bank developed from 1694 with just 19 staff to its present day form. Also, you can visit the shop and buy some unlikely Bank of England own-label products such as fridge magnets and, incredibly enough, claret and chardonnay.

Don't miss the 'Bank of England Today' section where you can impress your friends by making a quick fortune with some shrewd dealing on the FX Dealer simulation game.

And afterwards. . . If you've got time, your best bet is to cross Threadneedle Street and proceed down Cornhill where you will find several mysterious alleyways containing interesting drinking establishments. Simpsons Tavern is tucked away at the end of Ball Court. Along St. Michael's Alley, on the site of London's first coffee house (1652), is the Jamaica Wine House. This establishment has an interesting history which is documented in the front window display.

THE BANQUETING HOUSE
WHITEHALL PALACE

The Banqueting House

DRINKING, DRAMA, DECADENCE AND. . . DEATH

Whitehall, London, SW1A 2ER
Telephone: 020 7839 3787
Underground: Embankment, Westminster
Admission: £4.00 Concessions: £3.00 Children under 5 free, and up to 16 £2.60
Length of time required for visit: 45 mins
Open: 10am - 5pm Mon – Sat (sometimes closed for official functions)
Web site: www.hrp.org.uk

Directions
From Westminster tube station, take Exit 5 (Whitehall East), proceed along Parliament Street and then Whitehall. The Banqueting House is on the corner of Whitehall and Horse Guards Avenue. From Embankment station, take the Villiers Street exit and turn left into Embankment Place. Cross over to Whitehall Place, take the first left into Whitehall Court, turning right when you reach Horse Guards Avenue – the Banqueting House is on the corner at the end.

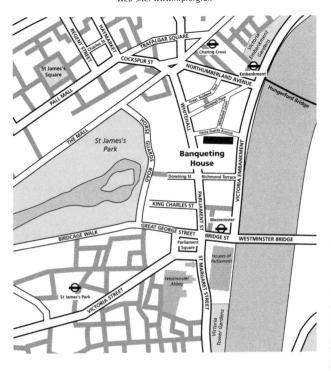

So. . . how would you spruce up your banqueting house? Well, in 1629, Charles I decided to bung Rubens a few grand and told him to 'do something with the ceiling'. The resultant masterpiece, now priceless, consisting of nine massive canvasses on a carved and ornate ceiling, is really quite breathtaking. It's a stunning glorification of the achievements of Charles I's father, James I – the monarch who commissioned the Banqueting House in the first place.

In those days the Banqueting House, designed by Inigo Jones, was a small part of Whitehall Palace, which was the sovereign's main residence from Henry VIII's time until it was destroyed by fire in 1698 – leaving the Banqueting House as the only remaining complete building.

Your tour starts below ground – in the undercroft – which was James I's drinking den. Here, a short video explains the history of the building after which you pick up your audio guide and move upstairs to the magnificent main hall.

As you move into the hall, your eyes are drawn upwards to the magnificent ceiling. The audio guide explains in detail all about the hall and how it would have been used for historic ceremonies, royal feasts, and extravagant court entertainment.

But it wasn't all fun and games here. In fact, this room is tinged with tragedy for it was here that Charles I met his death – the only British monarch ever to be executed. You can re-trace Charles I's last steps as he was led through the beautiful main hall to a specially constructed scaffold where a huge crowd was waiting. Here, on a cold winter morning in 1649, he was beheaded.

So, come and gaze in awe at the Rubens ceiling and find out more about the dramatic and tragic history of the Banqueting House.

And afterwards. . . There are two pubs located very near to the Banqueting House. When you leave, turn right and walk along Whitehall towards Trafalgar Square. After about 50 yards you will encounter The Clarence – a traditional pub with oak beams and wooden floors. Also, just a few doors away, you'll find The Old Shades – complete with wood panelling and a rather unusual domed ceiling.

The Barbican Art Gallery

ONE OF THE WONDERS OF THE MODERN WORLD. . .

Barbican Centre, Silk Street, London, EC2Y 8DS
Telephone: 020 7638 4141
Underground: Barbican, Moorgate
Admission: varies according to the exhibition Concessions: available
Length of time required for visit: 50mins
Open: 10am - 6pm Mon, Tue, Thu - Sat, 10am - 9pm Wed
12am - 6pm Sun & Bank Holidays
Web site: www.barbican.org.uk

Directions From Barbican tube station, follow the sign marked 'Footbridge to Barbican Centre' and have fun following the yellow signs along the elevated walkways. From Moorgate tube station, the Barbican centre is clearly sign-posted.

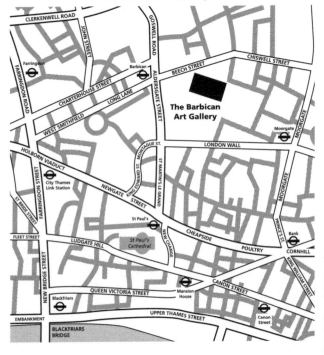

Owned, funded and managed by the Corporation of London, the Barbican Arts Centre is Europe's largest multi-arts and conference venue. It lies at the heart of the Barbican Complex – a mystifying labyrinth of high-level concrete walkways and residential areas that has 'Designed in the 1960s' stamped all over it.

In fact, it was planned in the 50s and 60s, built in the 70s and was opened by the Queen in 1982 who described it as 'One of the wonders of the modern world'. . . hmmmm, not quite sure about that one, ma'am.

Anyway, in the Arts Centre itself, we have two theatres, a concert hall, a public library, three cinemas, restaurants, shops and two art galleries – along with a sculpture hall and exhibition space. The centre also provides a home for both the London Symphony Orchestra and the Royal Shakespeare Company!

The two art galleries are well worth a visit, but you won't tend to find stuffy old masters on display here. Think more along the lines of challenging, entertaining, controversial, contemporary. Occasionally you might find that an exhibition is deemed to be 'unsuitable for young children' – for example, the recent Andres Serrano exhibition which featured startling and sometimes disturbing images (some of which involved the artist's own bodily fluids!).

There are also frequent free exhibitions, displays and sometimes music on the free stage. Admission to the Curve Gallery, on the ground floor, is usually free.

Worth phoning ahead to find out what's on.

And afterwards. . . If you're in need of fluid replacement, leave the centre via the Silk Street exit, turn left, and you can see the King's Head on the right – on the corner of Silk Street and Beech Street.

The Bramah Tea and Coffee Museum

FANCY A CUP OF GUNPOWDER?

40 Southwark Street SE1 1UN
Telephone: 020 7403 5650
Underground: London Bridge
Admission: £4.00 Concessions: £3.50
Length of time required for visit: 45mins
Open: 10am-6pm daily but closed 25-26 December
Web site: www.bramahmuseum.co.uk

Directions
From London
Bridge tube
station, take the
Borough High
Street (west side)
exit. When you
reach the High
Street, turn left.
Southwark Street
can be found a
short walk along –
where the main
road forks off to
the right.

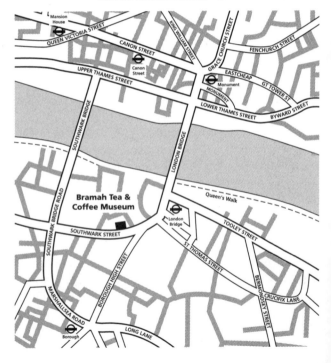

Mongolian Nomads, Opium Wars, the American War of Independence, Gina Lollobrigida. . . unlikely as it may seem, all these things form part of the colourful history of tea and coffee. But before we go on. . . tea bags and instant coffee? They get short shrift around here I'm afraid. . . these are the beverages of the devil! What we are celebrating here is the golden age of tea and coffee before those things were invented.

It's all explained here in Edward Bramah's wonderfully quaint and unusual museum – well really it's two museums in one. Your tour starts in the Tea Museum and after that you move on to the Coffee Museum which is in a separate building round the corner. And then, you get the chance to taste authentic leaf teas and aromatic roasted and ground coffees.

In the museums, the history of the two drinks going back over hundreds of years is explained in considerable detail. Of particular interest is London's role in all this (have a good look at Bramah's City Walk map) and the remarkable social changes that took place as the popularity of the drinks increased throughout the world.

And Edward Bramah himself? Well, he is an ex-tea planter, taster and collector and he founded the museum in 1992.

This is a homely, slightly quirky museum, packed with interesting items and information.

And it's not every day that you encounter the world's largest tea-pot!

And afterwards. . . By now you will be gagging for a taste of the real thing so you really must visit the museum café – no alcohol here but you have to try tea and/or coffee 'as it should be made'. You can have China Green Teas (including Gunpowder), China Black Teas, Indian, Japanese – remember to put the milk in the cup first and keep an eye on the tea-timer. There is also a range of wonderful coffees such as Kenyan, Colombian Excelso and Java Special.

The Britain at War Experience

PUT THOSE LIGHTS OUT!

64–66 Tooley Street, London Bridge, SE1 2TF
Telephone: 020 7403 3171
Underground: London Bridge, Monument
Admission: £6.50 Children: £3.50 Family Ticket: £15 Concessions: £4.50
Length of time required for visit: 1 hour
Open: 10am – 4:30pm daily (October – March), 10am – 5:30pm (April – September)
Web site: www.britainatwar.co.uk

Directions
From London Bridge tube station, take the Tooley Street exit. Turn right onto Tooley Street and the Britain at War Experience is about 50 yards along on the right. From Monument, cross over London Bridge on the left hand side and turn left at the end into Tooley Street – the Experience is about 100 yards along Tooley Street on the right.

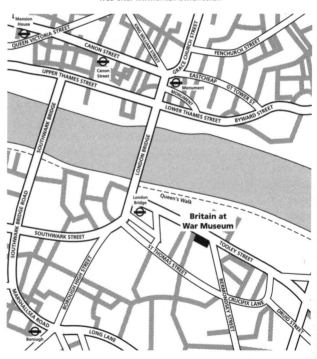

Britain 1939 – 1945. World War Two. Can you imagine what it must have been like to live in Britain during the war? Food rationing, clothes rationing, nightly air-raids, unexploded bombs, worldwide turmoil. . .

Well, the Britain at War Experience takes you back to war-torn Britain. But, as the name suggests, there is more to it than just showing photographs and displaying information. You really do experience it.

For example, you may have seen photographs of Andersen shelters erected in people's gardens as hideaways during air-raids. But, at the Britain at War Experience, you get the chance to huddle inside one, in the dark, with the terrifying sounds of an air-raid all around you.

This is just one of the many experiences that really capture the feel of living in Britain, especially London, during World War Two. There is also a wealth of interesting information along with rare documents and photographs – particularly relating to life in Southwark during the War.

The Britain at War Experience is not really about war as such – it's more about how the ordinary people coped while the war raged around them. This attraction is highly recommended and well worth a visit.

And afterwards. . . Handily placed, just a few doors away at 48-50 Tooley Street is Cooperage – a Davy's wine bar set beneath the railway arches with a mini-labyrinth of candlelit rooms. Here you will find excellent wines, food and Davy's Old Wallop served in pewter mugs. Or, for a more conventional English pub, the Barrow Boy and Banker can be found a short walk away – at the point where Borough High Street meets London Bridge.

The British Airways London Eye

IT'S EASY ON THE EYE!

Riverside Building, Westminster Bridge Road, SE1 7PB
Telephone: 0870 990 8881
Underground: Westminster, Waterloo
Admission: £9.50 Concessions: £8.50 Children: £5.00, under 5s free
Length of time required for visit: 50mins
Open: 9:30am – 10:00pm daily (May – September)
9.30am – 8:00pm daily (October – April) Closed January
Web site: www.british-airways.com/londoneye

Directions
From Westminster
Tube, cross over
the Thames via
Westminster
Bridge. From
Waterloo, take the
South Bank exit
and follow the
signs.

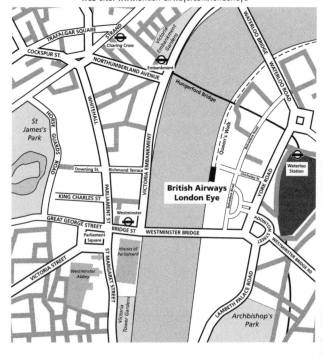

Late December 1999 and the outlook was a little bit grim for the London Eye – a few installation hiccups had occurred, the public were becoming increasingly sceptical and the press were ready to pounce. Then, at last, the Eye opened for business in February 2000. And with an eyebrow-raising 3.5 million visitors in its first year, the Eye has never looked back!

450 feet high, weighing 1500 tons and with a viewing distance of 25 miles, the Eye has proved to be a stunning addition to the London sky-line and it has firmly established itself as an enormously popular attraction.

And no wonder. The design of the Eye itself is quite magnificent and the whole thing is incredibly photogenic – especially at night. To really appreciate the size and design of the structure you should stand next to it and look up.

The capsules are also well designed and quite roomy – with space for about 25 people in each one. There's a bench in the middle of each capsule which is handy if you fancy a sit-down during your 30 minute flight.

The views? Stunning, spectacular, unforgettable – the capsule design allows you to see out from all sides giving amazing perspectives of London and its surroundings.

Due to the popularity of the Eye, it's best to book your flight in advance (and you can now do this on-line). You will be given a date and time for your flight and you're advised to turn up 30 minutes prior to your flight time in order to collect the tickets and board the Eye.

If you really want to splash out, you can book an entire capsule and for a truly unforgettable experience, why not have the champagne service with your own dedicated wine waiter!!

And afterwards. . . There are several options for 'back on firm ground' drinks in this area. There is Potters Bar located in the Travel Inn Capital (in the County Hall building). Failing that, in Chichely Street (just behind the 'Eye end' of County Hall) you will find an All Bar One with Bar Med right next door. For a more traditional pub, the Jubilee Tavern (which claims to be the 'closest pub to the Eye') is located in York Road (go to the end of Chichely Street and turn right).

The British Library

LITERARY TREASURES – AND SO MUCH MORE. . .

96 Euston Road, London, NW1 2DB
Telephone: 020 7412 7332
Underground: Kings Cross
Admission: Free
Length of time required for visit: 50mins – 1 hour
Open: 09:30 – 18:00 (Mon Wed Thu Fri) 09:30 – 20:00 (Tue)
09:30 – 17:00 (Sat) 11:00 – 17:00 (Sun and Bank Holidays)
Web site: www.bl.uk

Directions
From Kings Cross
tube, the British
Library is just a
short walk along
Euston Road
(north side)
beyond St.
Pancras station.

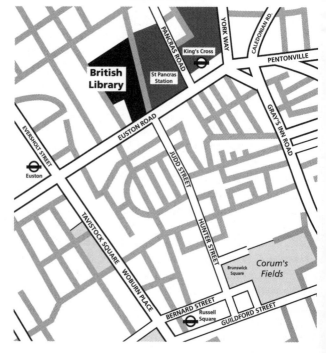

Okay, I hear you ask, why would you want to visit a library unless you intend to borrow a book? Well, we're not talking about some stuffy old civic building here – and you can't actually borrow books from here anyway. This is no ordinary library – in fact, the British Library's purpose-built home really is quite stunning and there is much for the visitor to see and do.

A few of the highlights are: the beautifully laid out piazza, the atmospheric John Ritblat Gallery and the restaurant and café overlooking the magnificently presented King's Library.

There are three exhibition galleries. The Workshop of Words, Sound and Images is an interactive gallery allowing hands-on activities often with demonstrations. The Pearson Gallery has special temporary exhibitions which allow various aspects of the collection to be shown and explained in more detail.

The John Ritblat Gallery really is a must-see for everyone – it's a permanent exhibition showing some of the greatest treasures of the British Library. A few of the many fascinating items are: the Magna Carta, Shakespeare's First Folio, Scott's Last Polar Journal, Nelson's last letter, a draft of the 1939 British ultimatum to Germany, many original manuscripts of famous writers. Also of interest are the vast and diverse sound archives – many of which can be heard on the numerous headphones that are provided. You can hear a wide range of things such as songs by the Beatles, the voice of Florence Nightingale from 1890, James Joyce reading an extract from Ulysses.

The King's Library is also a must-see. 65,000 volumes plus thousands more pamphlets and manuscripts all housed in a six-storey 17-metre glass-walled tower – which forms the centre-piece of the building.

And afterwards. . . Two suitable establishments can be found immediately opposite the front of the British Library. Firstly, there's the Euston Flyer, part of the Fullers Ale & Pie chain. Failing that, a few doors away, you can sample the craic at O'Neills Irish Bar.

The Cabinet War Rooms

BLOOD, TOIL, TEARS AND SWEAT. . .

Clive Steps, King Charles Street, London, SW1A 2AQ
Telephone: 020 7930 6961
Underground: Westminster, St. James's Park
Admission: £5.80 Concessions: £4.20
Length of time required for visit: 50mins
Open: 9:30am (10:00am 1 October – 31 March) to 6:00pm
Web site: www.iwm.org.uk

Directions
From Westminster tube station, the War Rooms are clearly signposted. From St. James Park tube station, exit onto Petty France. Cross over to Queen Anne's Gate and follow the signs to St. James Park. Turn right onto Birdcage Walk and after about 150 yards, turn left into Horse Guards Road. The War Rooms are about 150 yards on the right.

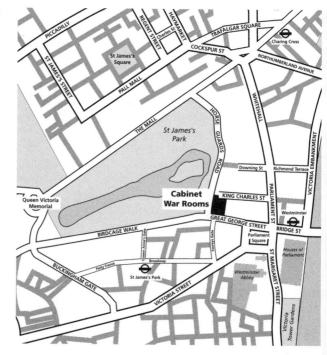

London 1940. Winston Churchill had just become Prime Minister but these were dark days for Britain – standing alone against the Nazis with the horrifying prospect of bombs raining down on the capital growing ever more likely.

So how could the top level Government officials and military personnel be protected while they directed the war effort? Well, to avoid giving the impression of deserting the public, they remained in Whitehall but went below ground – just 10 feet below ground in fact, in the converted and reinforced basement chambers of a Whitehall office building.

For the following six years, the Cabinet War Rooms were used as a top secret shelter for the central core of Government and military strategists. The main man in all this was the Prime Minister, Sir Winston Churchill.

Today you will find the War Rooms exactly as they were when the lights were switched off at the end of the war. You can see all the rooms and corridors as they were then – complete with maps, telephones and office equipment. You can see the Cabinet Room – laid out for a meeting of the Cabinet, the Transatlantic Telephone room – where Churchill had a hot-line to President Roosevelt and, of course, Churchill's room complete with his bed and nightshirt.

While much is made here of Churchill's character and the inspirational genius of his speeches, there is also an emphasis on how the lives of the less well known people who worked here must have been.

So, when Churchill came to power he offered nothing but 'blood, toil, tears and sweat'. . . come to the Cabinet War Rooms and experience the secret headquarters where he put it all into practise!

And afterwards. . . The Red Lion is handily placed – simply walk along King Charles Street (adjacent to the War Rooms entrance) and you will see the pub on the other side of Parliament Street. This pub stands on the site of a medieval tavern known in 1434 as the Hopping Hall – a detailed history can be found inside.

The Clink Prison Exhibition

PUT YOUR HEAD ON A REAL CHOPPING BLOCK!

1 Clink Street, SE1 9DG
Telephone: 020 7378 1558
Underground: London Bridge, Southwark
Admission: £4.00 Concessions: £3.00 Family Ticket: £9.00
Length of time required for visit: 30-45 minutes
Open: Winter: 10am-6pm Closed Christmas & New Year's Day. Summer: 10am-9pm
Web site: www.clink.co.uk

Directions
Exit London Bridge
tube station via
the Borough High
Street (west side)
exit. Walk straight
on and take the
first right into
Stoney Street. The
cobbled road of
Clink Street is at
the end of Stoney
Street. The
exhibition is about
50 yards on the
left along Clink
Street.

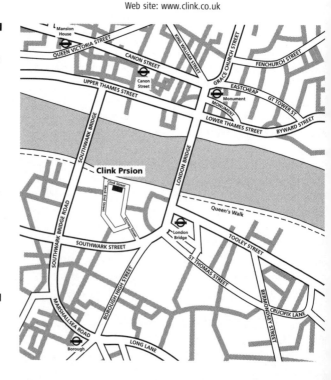

Sanctioning punishments and torture, licensing the brothels and stew-houses, regulating the theatres, bear-baiting pits and bowling alleys was all in a day's work for the Bishop of Winchester in the 14th century.

A strange job description for a member of the clergy you might think. Was it just unlucky or perhaps good fortune that the London Palace of the Bishop of Winchester was built in Southwark, just outside the gates and jurisdiction of the City of London, and all the activities that were banned within the city walls prospered just outside them!

The Clink Prison itself was burnt down during the Gordon Riots in 1780, and the only remaining part of the Palace is a 14th century rose window just up the road from the exhibition in Clink Street. However, inside the exhibition you can see the actual chopping blocks, axes and torture implements used in the Middle Ages, some of which need a bit of explaining, so if possible get a guided tour! Try them out for a fit, or imagine you're in one of the cells flooded by the tides of the Thames, you've got a bit of stretching on the rack to look forward to, and worse than all that you've got to share your cell with an out of work actor! It really does bring all those Blackadder and Monty Python sketches to life!

If you are a London Dungeon kind of person, then this exhibition is a must!

Note: Guided tours are available but it is advisable to book ahead before visiting.

And afterwards. . . The Market Porter is conveniently placed on the way back towards Borough High Street at 9 Stoney Street. The pub has a homely and friendly atmosphere and you may notice some slightly unusual opening hours. During the week, the doors open at 6:30 in the morning - to cater for the workers from Borough fruit and vegetable market .

Dali Universe

From Waterloo underground, take exit 6 and follow the signs to the South Bank (beyond the Waterloo International platform). Walk along the raised walkway and down the steps. Turn right at the bottom of the steps and right again following the signs for the Queen's Walk (Thames Path). Continue past the London Eye and the entrance to the Dali Universe is on your left in part of the County Hall building. From Westminster underground, take exit 1, cross Westminster Bridge, then take the first left onto the Thames Path, the Dali Universe is on your right past the London Aquarium.

TIME ON YOUR HANDS. . .?

County Hall, Riverside Building, Queen's Walk SE1 7PB
Telephone: 020 7620 2720
Underground: Waterloo, Westminster
Admission: £8.95 Concessions: £6.95 Under 10s are free, £4.95 for children over 10
Length of time required for visit: at least 1 hour
Open: Every day 10am-5.30pm, but closed 25 December
Web site: www.daliuniverse.com

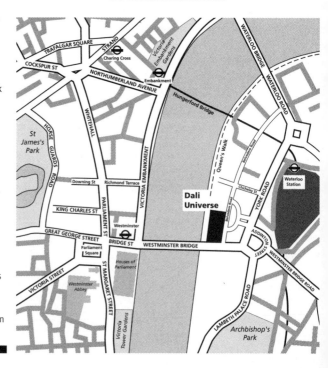

The 'Lobster Telephone', the 'Mae West Lips Sofa', the 'Space Venus', as well as hundreds of etchings and sculptures are all out on show here, at London's first permanent exhibition dedicated to the artistic genius Salvador Dali.

He once said 'The fact that I myself do not understand the meaning of my works at the time that I am painting them does not mean that they have no meaning'. Well, if he didn't understand them – what hope have we got! An hour or two could easily be spent just trying to figure out the meaning of one of his works, let alone the many artworks on view here. Luckily there are a few words of explanation along with each piece on display to make things a little easier.

You can also enjoy the many quotations written along the walkway before entering the gallery, which are as weird and wonderful and explicit as his artwork. There is Dali's version of the tarot cards (which you can buy in the shop afterwards), plenty of surreal furniture, lithographs, jewellery, and watercolours to ponder upon, and many television screens showing the artist, his work and his lifestyle.

In the basement there are often more artworks on display from a guest artist – just in case you have had your fill of melting clocks. So if the real world's getting you down, come and lose yourself in a surreal one at the Dali Universe.

And afterwards. . . Nearby pubs are given in the London Eye section.

Designmuseum

Design Museum

SLEEK LINES AND SEXY CURVES. . .

Butlers Wharf, 28 Shad Thames, SE1 2YD
Telephone: 020 7940 8790
Underground: Tower Hill, London Bridge
Admission: £6.00 Concessions: £4.00 Family of four: £16.00
Length of time required for visit: 50 mins – 1 hour
Open: 10.00am-5.45pm Mon-Sun
Web site: www.designmuseum.org

Directions
From Tower Hill tube station cross over Tower Bridge. The Design Museum is on the waterfront about 100 yards downstream of Tower Bridge. From London Bridge tube station, take the Tooley Street exit. Turn right and head for Hays Galleria, about 50 yards on the left. Walk through the Galleria and turn right onto Queens Walk (Thames Path). Walk along the waterfront to Tower Bridge where the museum is signposted.

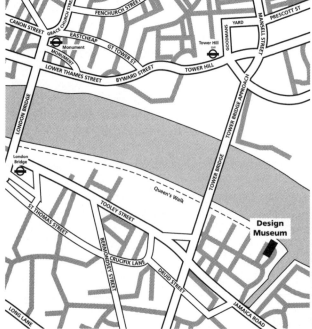

From toasters to 'Firebird' Gas Lighters, from cordless kettles to 'Lilliput' Salt and Pepper Shakers and from table lamps to 'Juicy Salif' Lemon Squeezers. From Aino Aalto to Kurt Ziehmer and from Alessi to Zanotta, welcome to the world of contemporary design.

This really is a museum with a difference. You won't find any relics of medieval London in this place – all the items on display are from the modern era. Here you will find out about the evolution of design and the inspiration behind the way things look and function. You will learn about design gurus such as Philippe Starck, Charles and Ray Eames, Frank Lloyd Wright and you will see how product design has shaped our culture.

The museum is housed in a bright and airy white-walled building which perfectly enhances the displays and exhibits. New themes, ideas and exhibits are regularly introduced so things are never static here.

The Collection Gallery illustrates the development of design in mass production and the Review Gallery displays some of the world's most innovative designs. The Temporary Gallery houses exhibitions which usually change every three months or so.

Also of considerable interest is the Design Museum shop offering a bewildering selection of classic and quirky design-related products – ideal for an unusual gift or souvenir of your visit.

And afterwards. . . Between the museum and Tower Bridge there are five excellent places for food and drink. For a quick drink and a bite to eat, your best bet is the All Bar One. If time is not pressing, try the Ask Restaurant or one of the three Conran establishments: the Cantina Del Ponte, Le Pont de la Tour, the Chop House and Bar.

The Dickens House Museum

GREAT EXPECTATIONS. . .

48 Doughty Street, London, WC1N 2LX
Telephone: 020 7405 2127
Underground: Kings Cross, Russell Square
Admission: £4.00 Concessions: £3.00
Length of time required for visit: 50mins – 1 hour
Open: 10am–5 pm Monday – Saturday; 11am-5pm Sundays
Web site: www.dickensmuseum.com

Directions
From Kings Cross tube, take the Gray's Inn Road exit – turn left at street level and head towards Gray's Inn Road. Walk down Gray's Inn Road until reaching Guilford Street – turn right into here and second left into Doughty Street. Dickens House is then about 50 yards away on the right. From Russell Square tube station, head to Guildford Street and turn left. As you pass Corum's Fields you'll see signposts for the museum.

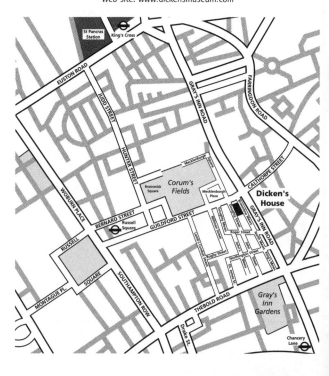

Ah yes, the large bottle full of blue ink, the quill pen, the pencil, the India rubber. . . and Charles Dickens working away at his desk creating characters such as Oliver Twist, Bill Sykes, the Artful Dodger and Nicholas Nickleby. It's all so easy to imagine here at Dickens House. Charles Dickens lived and worked in this house between 1837 and 1839 and it is his only London residence still standing today.

Mind you, Dickens' life wasn't always this cushy. You may be surprised to learn that when Dickens was 12, his father was sent to a debtors prison – in fact, the rest of the family went inside with him, while the young Dickens stayed alone in lodgings working in a warehouse.

However, in later years, the increasing success of his writing eventually enabled him to move to this Georgian terraced house in 1837. Today the house is packed full of Dickens related items and the Drawing Room has been restored to how it would have been in 1839.

You can see an iron grill from the Marshalsea Gaol that held his father all the way through to the writing desk on which Dickens wrote his last words. In between you can browse round the study in which Oliver Twist and Nicholas Nickleby were actually created.

And afterwards. . . Handily located just round the corner at 252 Gray's Inn Road, is the Calthorpe Arms. Owned by Youngs Brewery, this 'comfortable street-corner local' was recently named Pub of the Year by the North London branch of CAMRA. To find the pub, turn right on leaving Dickens House then first right towards Gray's Inn Road and the pub is on the opposite corner.

The Michael Faraday Laboratory and Museum

THE FATHER OF ELECTRICITY. . .

21 Albemarle Street, London, W1S 4BS
Telephone: 020 7409 2992
Underground: Green Park, Piccadilly Circus
Admission: £1.00 Concessions: £0.50
Length of time required for visit: 45 - 50mins
Open: 10:00am – 5:00pm Monday - Friday
Web site: www.ri.ac.uk

Directions
From Green Park tube, take the Piccadilly North Side exit and turn left at street level. Albemarle Street is about 5 minutes' walk on your left. From Piccadilly Circus tube, take the Piccadilly North Side exit and turn right at street level, Albemarle Street is about 7 minutes' walk on the right.

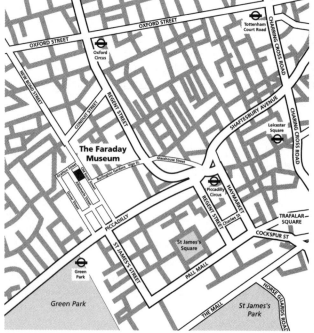

Diamagentism, colloidal suspensions, electro-magnetic induction. . . blimey, what's all this about? Well, it's all about Victorian scientific discovery and, in particular, the principles that led to the development of electric motors, generators and transformers.

What we have here, deep in the basement of the Royal Institution, is a restoration of Michael Faraday's Magnetic Laboratory on its original site.

Faraday first started working here as a lab assistant in 1813 and his scientific genius over the following 50 years led to world-changing discoveries in chemistry, electro-magnetic technology and electro-chemistry. Even now, generators in power stations are direct descendants from machines based on Faraday's first principles.

Today, you can come and visit his lab where you will see original apparatus and equipment, notebooks, manuscripts, testimonials and even the first sample of benzene - which he discovered.

So, next time you flick a light switch, perhaps you might just think of the pioneering genius of Michael Faraday – toiling away in his Victorian laboratory.

And afterwards. . . Buzz back towards Piccadilly along Albemarle Street and you will find 'heritage and hospitality' at Shelleys. Also handily placed (in Stafford Street) is the Duke of Albemarle – where you can see the original Stafford Street Stone from 1686.

The Golden Hinde

SCURVY, MUTINY, PIRACY AND PLUNDER. . .

St Mary Overie Dock, Cathedral Street, SE1 9DE
Telephone: 08700 11 8700
Underground: London Bridge, Monument
Admission: £2.50 Concessions: £2.10
Length of time required for visit: 30mins
Open: 9am-sunset daily (worth calling ahead to check)
Web site: www.goldenhinde.co.uk

Directions
From London Bridge tube station, take either the Duke Street Hill exit of the Tooley Street exit. At street level, turn left and you will see Southwark Cathedral on the other side of the main road. The Golden Hinde is on the waterfront to the left of the cathedral. From Monument, walk over London Bridge on the right hand side and you will see the ship from the bridge.

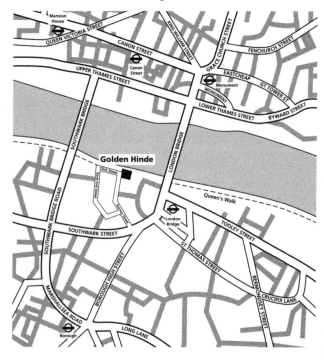

In 1577 Francis Drake was asked by Queen Elizabeth I to explore the ocean that lay on the other side of South America. During his expedition, Drake became the first Englishman to navigate the Straits of Magellan. He survived a mutiny, and also accumulated vast amounts of booty by raiding Spanish ships and settlements. Unable to find a way back to the Atlantic, he sailed West and eventually headed homewards via the Cape of Good Hope. Three years later and Drake and his galleon, *The Golden Hinde*, were back – having circumnavigated the world.

Not long after his return, the Queen came aboard the Golden Hinde, on the Thames at Deptford, and Drake was awarded a knighthood.

The Golden Hinde that is available for boarding at St. Marie Overie Dock, near to London Bridge, is a meticulous reconstruction of Drake's original. This version of the Golden Hinde, however, is not just a mock-up. In fact, she has herself completed a circumnavigation and has sailed over 140,000 miles. Since her launch in the early 1970s she has acted as a floating museum in countless numbers of ports all round the world.

You can explore her five decks accompanied by various crew members (dressed in period clothes) and find out, at first hand, how life would have been on an Elizabethan warship.

So, climb aboard and try to imagine how it must have been with 100 men on board, sailing through un-chartered waters, heavily laden with plundered treasure. . .

And afterwards. . . Handily placed right next to the Golden Hinde is The Old Thameside Inn. This pub was once a spice warehouse and has a large outdoor seating area overlooking the Thames.

The Guards Museum

CHARGE YOUR MUSKET!

Wellington Barracks, Birdcage Walk, London, SW1E 6HQ
Telephone: 020 7414 3271
Underground: St James's Park
Admission: £2.00 Concessions: £1.00 Children free
Length of time required for visit: 40 - 50mins
Open: 10am - 4pm daily (closed on some ceremonial days)
Web site: www.army.mod.uk/ceremonialandheritage/museums/details/m094guar.htm

Directions
From St. James's Park tube, exit on to Petty France. Cross over to Queen Anne's Gate and follow the sign to St. James's Park. This brings you out on to Birdcage Walk – turn left and the museum is about 75 yards along on the left.

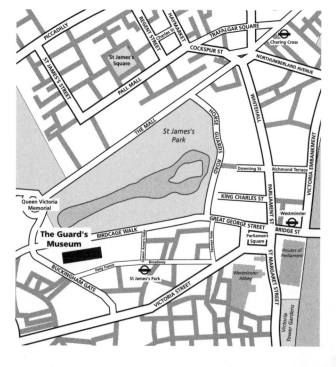

The bright red tunics, the huge bearskins, the crowds of tourists peering through the railings at Buckingham Palace. . . most of us are familiar with the trappings of the Changing of the Guards. But not many of us are aware of the history that lies behind this popular ceremonial event and in particular the details and origins of the Guards themselves.

Well, just a short walk away from the hubbub of Buckingham Palace, you will find the small but informative Guards Museum. This fascinating museum attempts to tell the story of the Foot Guards largely through displays and stories about the individuals who helped shaped the history of the five regiments of Foot Guards: Grenadier, Coldstream, Scots, Irish and Welsh.

The origins of the Foot Guards go all the way back to the turbulent times of the English Civil War. Back in 1651 things were looking a bit on the bleak side for the monarchy and royalists in general – Cromwell was firmly in charge, Charles I had been executed and Charles II was now forced out of the country. Charles II needed guarding during his nine-year exile and during this period and his subsequent restoration we start to see the first manifestations of the Grenadier Guards, Coldstream Guards and Scots Guards. The Irish and Welsh Guards were formed much later (1900 and 1914).

So, the museum initially takes you back to the dramatic mid-1600s. You'll find out about pikemen, musketeers, halberds and spontoons. Not to mention how to shoulder your pike, charge your musket and withdraw your scouring stick. There are also objects and displays relating to 18th Century London, the Battle of Waterloo, the Crimean War all the way through to World War Two and the post-war period.

And the bearskins? Well, don't worry, they no longer shoot bears in order to make them! Apparently they are almost indestructible and there are plenty to go round. . .

And afterwards. . . Turn right on leaving the museum and march along Birdcage Walk. After about 75 yards, turn right into Queen Anne's Gate where you will see the Old Star immediately opposite the tube station. Here you will find suitable refreshments along with some very tasty options on the 'Pizza in the Pub' menu.

39

The Guildhall and Guildhall Art Gallery

AND YE BONUS BALL IS. . .

Guildhall Yard, off Gresham Street, London, EC2V 5AE
Telephone: Guildhall 020 7606 3030, Art Gallery: 020 7332 3700
Underground: Bank
Admission: Guildhall Free, Art Gallery £2.50 Concessions: £1.00 Children free
Prebooked parties of 10 or more £2 Free after 3.30pm and all day Friday
Length of time required for visit: 50mins – 1 hour
Open: Guildhall 10am – 5pm Monday – Sunday (May – September)
10am – 5pm Monday – Saturday (October – April)
Art Gallery: 10am – 5pm Monday – Saturday 12am – 4pm Sunday
Web site: www.cityoflondon.gov.uk, www.guildhall-art-gallery.org.uk

Directions
From Bank tube
station, take exit
1 – the Guildhall
is well signposted.

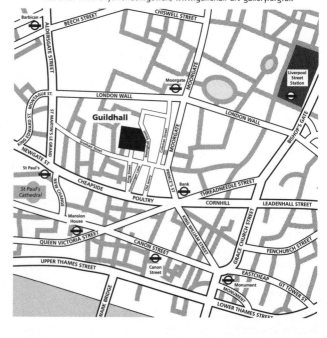

The trial of Lady Jane Grey (1553), the 17th century lottery show, lavish celebrations following the defeat of Napoleon (1815). . . all the way through to the bestowing of the freedom of the city on Nelson Mandela (1996) – just a few of the ceremonial events that have taken place here at the Guildhall.

The Guildhall is the home of the Corporation of London, but it was only built in the 1400s and the City of London has been governed from this site ever since Saxon times – over 800 years. You can visit the Great Hall, where the events listed above took place, with its oak-panelled roof, decorative windows, minstrels' gallery and monuments. Many state trials took place here and several of them are listed on a tablet on the north wall – including that of Nicholas Throckmorton who, in 1554, was found not guilty but the verdict was considered unsatisfactory so the jury were sent to prison!

And afterwards. . . Off Basinghall Street (adjacent to the Guildhall) you will find a small alley called Masons Avenue. Here you will find the 17th century pub The Old Doctor Butlers Head.

There is also the 15th century porch and the largest medieval crypt in London. Please note that the Great Hall and the crypt are actually working buildings and, as such, are sometimes not open to the public – so phone first to check.

Also on this site is the Guildhall Art Gallery – where the Corporation's collection, going as far back as the 16th century, is housed. The collection is now in a superb purpose-built gallery – which was opened in 1999 allowing public viewing for the first time since the original gallery was destroyed in World War Two. There are many highlights – including famous Pre-Raphaelite works and London subjects from the 17th Century to the present day. Also, there is the huge 'Copley Painting' – measuring a gigantic 5.5m by 7.5m. This is one of the country's largest oil paintings. It has remained hidden from public view for over 50 years due to the lack of a wall big enough to hang it!

HMS Belfast

FROM THE ARCTIC TO THE FAR EAST

Morgans Lane, Tooley Street, SE1 2JH
Telephone: 020 7940 6300
Underground: London Bridge, Tower Hill
Admission: £5.80 Concessions: £4.40 Children under 16 free (but must be supervised)
Length of time required for visit: 1 hour
Open: Mar-Oct 10am-6pm daily Nov-Feb 10am-5pm daily
Web site: www.iwm.org.uk/belfast

Directions
From Tower Hill tube station, head for Tower Bridge. When crossing Tower Bridge you see will see HMS Belfast on your right. From London Bridge tube station, take the Tooley Street exit. Turn right and follow signs to Hays Galleria – walk through the Galleria towards Queen's Walk (Thames Path).

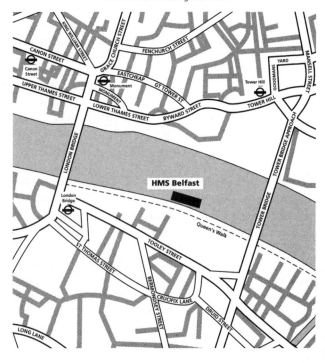

Magnetic mine attacks, WWII Arctic convoys, the Normandy Landings, the Korean War, guns trained on an M1 service area, mad reindeers. . . yes, HMS *Belfast* has seen it all during her rich and varied career.

First launched in 1938, HMS *Belfast*'s operational life lasted until 1965 and then, instead of heading for the scrap yard, she became a unique floating museum of twentieth century naval heritage. This 10,000 tonne battle cruiser now forms an unmistakable part of the Thames between London Bridge and Tower Bridge.

Having served throughout the Second World War she then went on to support United Nations forces in Korea. After that she continued with peacetime duties in the Far East and was then brought to London and opened to the public on Trafalgar Day in 1971.

Today, HMS *Belfast* is still living a comparatively quiet life providing entertainment for her many thousands of visitors. You can tour all round the nine decks where you will see the bridge, the quarterdeck, the gun turrets. Visit the Messdecks and gain a fascinating insight into what life must have been like for the crew. Don't miss the rather eerie radio-room re-enactment of a real life engagement – namely, the sinking of the battle cruiser *Scharnhorst* during World War Two.

And the reindeer? Well, the unfortunate animal was presented as a mascot for the crew but was eventually driven mad by the confinement. . .

And afterwards. . . If you've got time, The Horniman is very handily placed right by the entrance to HMS *Belfast*. You can obtain a drink from the bar and then take it outside and watch the Thames go by. The pub itself commemorates the travels and trade of F.J. Horniman, the Victorian tea importer who landed his tea here.

ENGLISH HERITAGE

The Jewel Tower

A BRANCH OF THE KING'S PRIVY WARDROBE. . .

Abingdon Street, London, SW1P 3JY
Telephone: 020 7222 2219
Underground: Westminster
Admission: £1.60 Concessions: £1.20 Children: £0.80, under 5s free
Length of time required for visit: 50mins
Open: 1 Apr – 30 Sep: 10am – 6pm daily, 1 Oct – 31 Oct: 10am – 5pm daily
1 Nov – 31 Mar: 10am – 4pm daily

Directions
From Westminster
tube, take exit 5.
At street level turn
towards the
Houses of
Parliament. Cross
over Bridge Street
with the Houses
of Parliament on
your left – the
Jewel Tower is
about 100 yards
further on, on the
right-hand side of
the road.

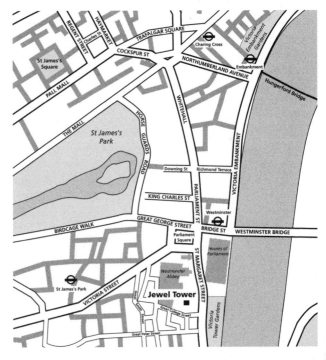

1365 at the Palace Of Westminster – Edward the Third finds himself surrounded by more jewellery, pomp and splendour than he can cope with. Being slightly short of storage space (due to the weaponry required for the French War), he decides to build himself a second Privy Wardrobe in the form of an 'L'-shaped building, now known as the Jewel Tower.

Now, by today's standards, it's not much of a tower and there aren't actually any jewels anymore, but the Jewel Tower is an intriguing little site in amongst the big boys of Westminster Abbey and the Houses of Parliament.

You may not realise this but there was a 500-year period (until Henry the Eighth's reign) when the Kings of England had their main residence at Westminster and the Jewel Tower is, in fact, one of the least altered buildings to have survived from the days of the medieval palace.

Today, the 'L'-shaped tower, the moat and the site of the palace garden can all be explored. You can find out all about the history of the building and the old palace. Inside the tower itself, you will find the History of Parliament exhibition – a detailed account of the growth and development of Parliament along with a video of Parliament in action.

And afterwards. . . Climbing the stone spiral staircase will no doubt have left you gasping for refreshments – the nearest pub is not far away in the shape of the Westminster Arms at 9 Storey's Gate. The best way to get here is to head back in the direction of Westminster tube but turn left into the footpath by St. Margaret's Church – go past the front of Westminster Abbey and cross over to Storey's Gate.

Dr Johnson's House

FOR THERE IS IN LONDON ALL THAT LIFE CAN AFFORD. . .

17 Gough Square, Fleet Street, London, EC4A 3DE
Telephone: 020 7353 3745
Underground: Blackfriars, Chancery Lane
Admission: £4.00 Concessions: £3.00 Children: £1.00 Family ticket: £9.00
Length of time required for visit: 50mins
Open: 11am – 5:30pm Monday – Saturday (May to September)
11am – 5:00pm Monday – Saturday (October – April) Closed Bank Holidays
Web site: www.drjh.dircon.co.uk

Directions
From Blackfriars tube, take the Ludgate Circus exit and head along New Bridge Street towards Ludgate Circus – you will find signposts to Dr Johnson's House when you reach Fleet Street (on your left). From Chancery Lane, take exit 3 for Fleet Street and head towards Holborn Circus – signposts start when you reach New Fetter Lane.

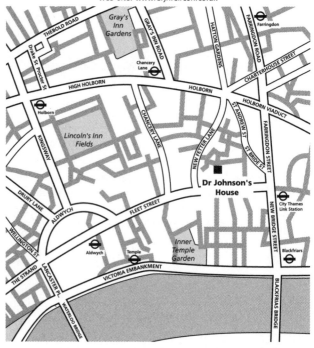

Dr. Samuel Johnson – Dictionary Johnson, the Oracle of Fleet Street – a larger-than-life character and the compiler of the first comprehensive English dictionary. Johnson, variously described as 'huge, shambling, thunderous of voice', lived and worked in this house from 1748 until 1759. This is Johnson's only known surviving residence and is where he compiled most of the famous dictionary.

Johnson's work introduced a new standard to the compilation of dictionaries and incorporated, for the first time, many of the features that are still evident in modern day dictionaries. But Johnson was also known as a great speaker with a cutting sense of humour – which often carried over in to his dictionary. Who else would describe Oats as 'a grain which in England is generally given to horses, but in Scotland supports the people' or how about: Excise Duty. . . 'a hateful tax levied by wretches hired by those to whom excise is paid'.

The house itself was restored and opened to the public in 1911 by Lord Harmsworth – who was keen that it should not be turned into an 'old curiosity shop' full of 'irrelevant bric-a-brac'. The house has been restored to how it was during Johnson's time with period furniture, first editions of the Dictionary, letters, prints and portraits. There is also an excellent video presentation in which the ghosts of Dr. Johnson and his biographer, James Boswell, meet and discuss the house and Johnson's life.

And afterwards. . . One of the many lanes and courts surrounding the house is Wine Office Court. Here you will find a further taste of a bygone age at Ye Olde Cheshire Cheese – one of London's few remaining 17th Century Chop Houses. The pub boasts an impressive list of famous patrons including Charles Dickens and, of course, Dr. Johnson himself!

LONDON AQUARIUM

FLOOD YOUR SENSES

Directions
From Waterloo underground, take exit 6 and follow the signs to the South Bank (beyond the Waterloo International platform). Walk along the raised walkway and down the steps. Turn right at the bottom and right again following the signs for Queen's Walk (Thames Path). Continue past the London Eye and the Aquarium is on your left. From Westminster underground, take exit 1, cross Westminster Bridge, take the first left onto the Queen's Walk, and the Aquarium is on your right.

London Aquarium

TAKE A WALK ON THE WET SIDE. . .

County Hall, Westminster Bridge Road, SE1 7PB
Telephone: 020 7967 8007
Underground: Waterloo, Westminster
Admission: £8.75 Concessions: £6.50 Children 3-14 £5.25, unders 3s free
Family Ticket: £25
Length of time required for visit: 1 hour upwards
Open: Every day 10am-6pm
Web site: www.londonaquarium.co.uk

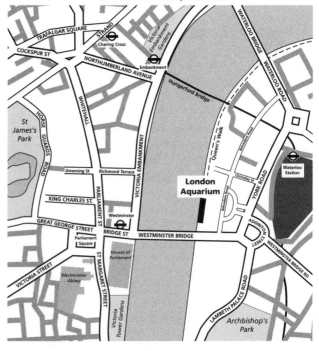

Gigantic tube worms, football-sized clams, and blind crabs – no it's not time for a medical dictionary – it's time to find out more at the London Aquarium!

This is housed in what was County Hall, built originally as the headquarters for the London County Council, the forerunner of the GLC, and is now home itself to all sorts of interesting creatures.

Sitting on the bank of the river Thames it is appropriate that the tour (either guided or at your own pace) starts off with the natural history of the Thames, and the not-so-natural history – use your imagination here. Then you are taken to the relative comfort of a freshwater environment, but before you know it you are heading straight towards the giant Atlantic aquarium with sharks and conger eels hiding behind every rock.

Then from the colour of the Pacific and Indian oceans, you are taken to the depths of an abyss to experience what it's like 7 miles down in the Mariana trench. There are also freshwater rivers and ponds, mangrove swamps, tropical and coral reef aquariums to explore. There's plenty of time to admire the terrapins, wonder why lobsters have blue blood, or just shiver at the thought of meeting a piranha.

You can watch the sharks being fed, let your fingers feel the rays or just come face to face with a jellyfish or two. They are all here. So if you're fed up with all those city sharks, then come and see some real ones here at the London Aquarium.

And afterwards. . . Nearby pubs are listed in the London Eye section.

The London Dungeon

THE ULTIMATE HORROR EXPERIENCE

28-34 Tooley Street, SE1
Telephone: 09 001 600 066
Underground: London Bridge
Admission: £9.50 (group rates available) Concessions: £6.50
Students: £8.25 Children: 4-14 £6.50
Length of time required for visit: 2 hours
Open: 10am-6pm Apr-Sep, 10.30am-5pm Oct-Mar
Web site: www.thedungeons.com

Directions
From London
Bridge tube
station take the
Tooley Street exit.
Turn right along
Tooley Street and
the entrance to
the London
Dungeon is about
50 yards on your
right in a railway
arch.

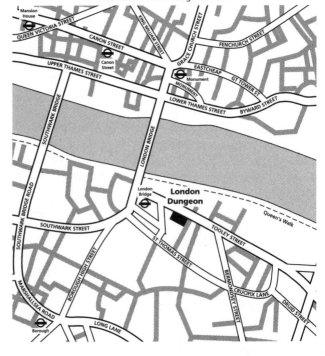

Death, damnation, torture, disease, blood, guts and gore... oh, and a roller-coaster boat ride. Its all here! Basically, anything ghastly that has happened in British history is on view here. No holds barred. If gruesome and grisly displays are your cup of tea, this is the place to come.

How about experiencing the Great Fire of London in the lifesize reconstruction of Pudding Lane, or you can take a one-way boat-ride down the River Thames towards the infamous 'Traitors Gate' entrance to the Tower of London, and then meet your personal executioner! You can walk down the tiny, crowded, plague-infested streets of London in the 1600s, experience a medieval siege, or just visit the good old torture chamber!

You can see how imaginative our predecessors were when it came to torturing prisoners, or executing the guilty parties. Find out what being 'hung, drawn and quartered' really meant, what an 'iron maiden' was long before heavy metal rock bands were thought of, or perhaps the latest vogue in chastity belts!

The London Dungeon has on display all the horrors in our history from torture, imprisonment, executions, murders, witchcraft, sacrifices, the ravages of the plague; even the exploits of Jack the Ripper are portrayed. Strangled moans and cries, in true Hammer House of Horror style accompany your walk throughout the dungeon, along with the odd costumed actor who might spring out on you. . . so beware!

This is more like 'London in an Afternoon', or perhaps a Friday lunchtime! It is best avoided during the busy summer months, but from September through to May you can generally walk straight in, if school holidays are avoided.

And afterwards. . . The nearby bar 'Skinkers' is recommended as it is virtually next door to the Dungeon on Tooley Street, almost opposite the entrance to Hays Galleria.

The
M NUMENT
Great Fire of London 1666

The Monument

FANCY A WORKOUT? ONLY 311 STEPS TO CLIMB!

Monument Street, London EC3 8AH
Telephone: 020 7626 2717
Underground: Monument
Admission: £1.50 Children: £0.50
Length of time required for visit: 25-30 mins
Open: 9.30am - 5:00pm Daily

Directions
From Monument underground station, turn right from the main exit – the Monument is slap bang in front of you!

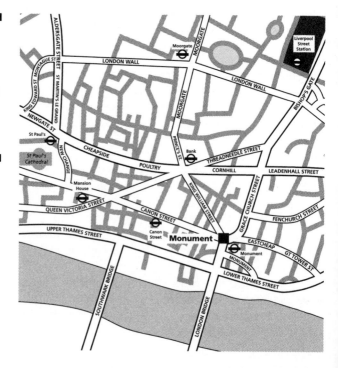

Sunday September 2nd 1666. A baker in Pudding Lane decides that some fresh cakes would be in order. Three days later and not only are his cakes over-done but the resultant Great Fire of London has destroyed most of the City. Cor blimey, strike a light.

Now this wasn't as bad as it sounds. Firstly, there was surprisingly little loss of life and secondly, the fire ended the worst ravages of the plague.

Obviously the damage to vast number of houses, streets, public buildings and churches was severe. In 1677, as part of the re-building programme, the 202-foot-tall Monument to the Great Fire was completed. People have been visiting the Monument for over three hundred years!

Designed by Sir Christopher Wren, it's the tallest free-standing stone column in the world.

Now, although it is not obvious to the passer-by, inside this enormous structure is a stone staircase that spirals all the way up to an open-air viewing platform at the top of the column. From here, there are wonderful views of London, although the days when this was the tallest structure in this area are long since gone.

Be warned though, it's quite a steep and narrow climb to the top – best to avoid wearing high-heeled shoes if you intend to give it a go.

When you eventually clamber down, you will be presented with a very nice and official-looking certificate to signify that you have climbed the 311 steps of the Monument.

And afterwards. . . Time permitting, you can quench your thirst and study your certificate in detail at The Hogshead – handily located about 25 yards from the entrance to the Monument.

A regular feature at the Hogshead is the week-long Beer Festival where there are upwards of 50 guest ales to choose from – so you can combine your visit to the Monument with a taste of Bunce's Pigswill or Rooster's Cream (or whatever you fancy).

The Museum of London

WHAT LIES BENEATH YOUR FEET?

150 London Wall, EC2Y 5HN
Telephone: 020 7600 3699
Underground: Barbican, St Paul's
Admission: Free
Length of time required for visit: 1 hour upwards
Open: 10am-5.50pm Mon-Sat, 12-5.50pm Sun
Web site: www.museumoflondon.org.uk

Directions
From St. Paul's underground, take exit 1 and head up St Martins-Le-Grand until you meet London Wall. From the Barbican underground head down Aldersgate Street until you meet London Wall. The museum is a modern building and the main entrance is above street level, so follow the signs.

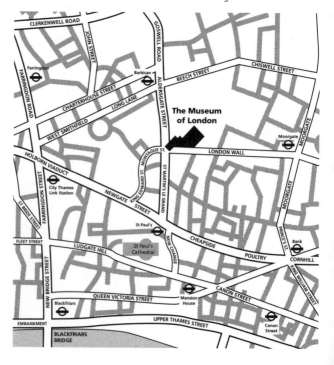

London: it's warm, dry and sunny. The locals are scantily clad in furs, and lazing about on the banks of a picturesque river, consuming shellfish and game for their dinner. No, it's not the latest trendy café or Millennium project, and surely it can't be the river Thames. . .or London. . .or England, that's being described. But it was, just a cool 400,000 years ago! It seems a lot more idyllic than today's frantic existence in the capital.

Just think! Beneath all the modern buildings or your feet as you read this, could be Roman coin hoards, forgotten graveyards, bodies, mummified cats, pottery, jewellery, and even the latest in Roman waste disposal design! They've all been found here, so instead of getting your metal detector out of retirement pop along to The Museum of London to find out more. Basically if something of interest has been dug up in London, chances are it's on display here.

This museum, as its name suggests, details the entire history of the development of London, from earliest prehistoric times half a million years ago, right up until the present day. The different periods in history are exhibited in galleries, so you can wander through time, or fast forward to your favourite era. The displays take the form of archaeological finds, paintings, text, prints, photographs and reconstructions. Not only is there all this to absorb, but there are temporary exhibitions as well. It is definitely worth timing your visit with one of these.

It is easy to while away a lunchtime in just one of the galleries, so now it's free, you can pop in as often as you like.

And afterwards. . . The Lord Raglan is a traditional city pub situated between the museum and St. Paul's tube station on St. Martins-Le-Grand. It celebrates the Commander-in-Chief of the Crimean Campaign.

National Gallery

The National Gallery

BRUSH UP ON THE OLD MASTERS. . .

Trafalgar Square, London, WC2N 5DN
Telephone: 020 7747 2885
Underground: Leicester Square, Charing Cross
Admission: Free
Length of time required for visit: 50mins (for quick tour)
Open: 10am - 6pm daily (Wednesday until 9pm)
Web site: nationalgallery.org.uk

Directions

From Leicester Square tube, take the Charing Cross Road South exit and turn left at street level. The National Gallery overlooks Trafalgar Square which is about 5 or 6 minutes' walk down Charing Cross Road on the right. From Charing Cross Tube, take the Trafalgar Square exit - at street level, turn to the right and you are now facing the National Gallery.

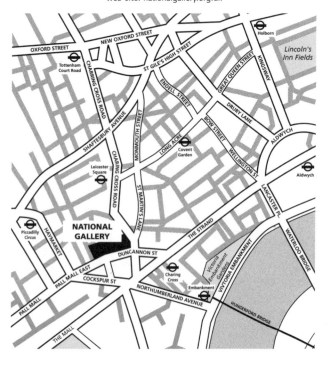

Da Vinci, Michelangelo, Rembrandt, Constable, Van Gogh. . . yes they're all here as part of one of the finest collections of Western European paintings in the world. And it's all free!

What you have here is over 2,000 paintings by all the European greats – dating from the 13th Century to the early 20th Century.

Now, obviously, the Gallery is massive and you may need a plan in order to make the most of your visit. We suggest that, on arrival, you should pick up a free floor plan from the Information Desks. You can visit the Micro Gallery to devise your own guided tour or use the Gallery Guide Sound Track audio system and follow the highlights tour. Both allow you to establish quickly the location of the most famous paintings and, before you know it, you will have seen and learnt all about many of the world's greatest masterpieces. Botticelli's 'Venus and Mars', Constables 'Hay Wain', Van Gogh's 'Sunflowers'. . . the list is endless.

Entrance is free but don't forget to make a donation!

And afterwards. . . No doubt the simmering heat of Seurat's 'Bathers at Asnieres' will have left you needing a drink. If so, in nearby St. Martin's Lane you will find The Salisbury – which claims to be 'London's most magnificently preserved historic drinking house.' Here you can enjoy hand-carved mahogany splendour while quenching your thirst and discussing the National Gallery classics.

NATIONAL
PORTRAIT
GALLERY

The National Portrait Gallery

ALL THOSE FAMOUS MUG-SHOTS!

St Martin's Place, London, WC2H 0HE
Telephone: 020 7306 0055
Underground: Leicester Square, Charing Cross
Admission: Free
Length of time required for visit: 1 hour
Open: 10am-6pm daily (until 9pm Thursday and Friday)
Web site: www.npg.org.uk

Directions
From Leicester Square tube, take the Charing Cross Road South exit and turn left at street level. The National Portrait Gallery is about 5 minutes' walk down Charing Cross Road on the right. From Charing Cross tube, take the Trafalgar Square exit. At street level, turn to the right and you are facing the National Gallery – the National Portrait Gallery entrance is round to the right of the National Gallery.

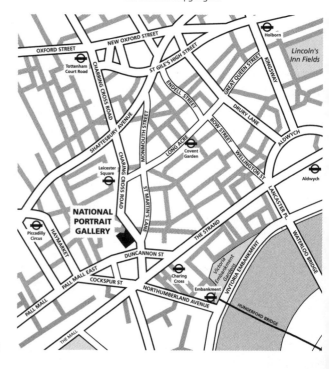

Give me British warriors, statesmen, artists, writers and scientists. . . but make sure they're all dead! Back in 1856, this was the basic criteria for a portrait to be allowed entry in to the National Portrait Gallery's collection. In those days, the Gallery didn't have a permanent home and was moved round London for the next 40 years until finally arriving at its current location in 1896 – attracting 4,200 visitors on its opening day.

Today's Gallery attracts 1 million visitors a year and has many thousands of portraits ranging from the Chandos portrait of Shakespeare (the first portrait given to the Gallery) all the way through to modern day pop and sports stars. It's basically a massive who's who of Britain's most famous.

The Gallery is arranged in chronological order with the bulk of the portraits spread over 3 floors. Starting from the top, the second floor houses 1505 – 1837, the first floor has the Victorians to the late 20th century and the ground floor has Britain since 1990. There are frequent exhibitions, events and lectures.

Also of note is the IT Gallery. Here you will find touch-screen computers allowing you to create your own personal tour by adding portraits to a personal tour map. When you're ready, simply press Print and you have a tour map tailored to your own requirements!

So come and see the people who have made us what we are today! From William Shakespeare to Elizabeth Taylor, from Henry VIII to David Beckham. . . and who knows, one day you might just find your own portrait on display!

Note: There are a series of lunchtime lectures. See the web site for more details.

And afterwards. . . Very handily placed (and aptly named) just over the road from the Gallery is the Chandos. Head upstairs to the Opera Bar and if you're lucky you can relax on a Chesterfield sofa while enjoying the reasonably priced beer.

Florence Nightingale Museum

WE ARE STEEPED UP TO OUR NECKS IN BLOOD. . .

2 Lambeth Palace Road, London, SE1 7EW
Telephone: 020 7620 0374
Underground: Westminster, Waterloo
Admission: £4.80 Concessions: £3.80 Special group rates for 11 or more
Length of time required for visit: 50mins - 1 hour
Open: Mon - Fri 10:00 - 17:00, Sat & Sun 11:30 - 16:30
Web site: www.florence-nightingale.co.uk

Directions

From Westminster Tube, take Exit 3 and walk over Westminster Bridge. There are signs for the Museum at St Thomas's Hospital. From Waterloo, take the South Bank exit from the main station concourse and walk over the footbridge. Go down the steps on the left immediately before the Shell Centre to York Road. At the end of York Road (2/3 minutes) you will see the museum sign at St Thomas's Hospital on the opposite side of the road.

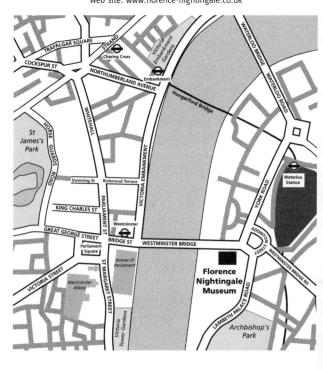

The voice of God, the Crimean War, the Lamp. . . all part of the Florence Nightingale legend. But there's so much more! Let's add heroine, humanitarian, reformer, writer, statistician – to name but a few. The achievements of FN are, quite simply, immense and they are all wonderfully presented in this fascinating museum.

Did you know that FN originally left a high society background to train as a nurse at a time when all nurses were merely regarded as 'drunken and promiscuous'? Did you know that as well as instigating professional training for nurses she was also an army health reformer, a hospital reformer, a brilliant and innovative statistician – in 1860 she became the first woman Fellow of the Statistical Society.

Well, the museum takes you step by step through FN's life and uses a variety of methods to explain each extraordinary chapter. Her work in the Crimea and the horrors of Scutari Hospital – her most famous period – are depicted in powerful detail. There are original objects, visual displays, reconstructions and an excellent audio-visual presentation in a small cinema.

So, come and find out more about FN – one of the most influential women of the 19th century. And, what's more, you can even see one of the original lamps that she carried!

And afterwards. . . Well, if all that work packed into one incredible life has left you feeling thirsty, you won't need a lamp to guide you across Lambeth Palace Road to 199 Westminster Bridge Road, where you will find the Florence Nightingale pub! The pub is slightly tucked away in a corner to the left of York House.

The Old Bailey

HANG 'EM HIGH!

Old Bailey, EC4M
Telephone: 020 7248 3277
Underground: St. Paul's
Admission: Free
Length of time required for visit: 30 minutes
Open: 10.30am-1pm, 2pm-4.30pm Mon-Fri, and closed all public holidays
Web site: no official - try www.thisislondon.co.uk

Directions
Take exit 1 from
St. Paul's
underground, and
turn left along
Newgate Street.
Keep going until
you meet a road
called Old Bailey.
Turn left down
here and the
entrance to the
public galleries of
the Central
Criminal Courts is
on your left down
an alleyway called
Warwick Passage.

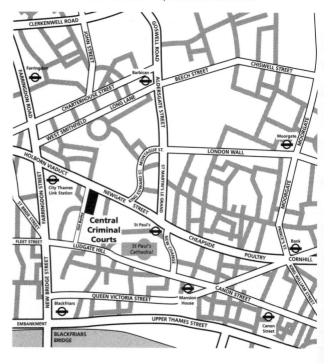

'The most notorious of criminals, the most odious of crimes and the finest of judges', have all made their way to the Old Bailey. Now it's your turn!

The Central Criminal Court, nicknamed the Old Bailey just from the name of the street in which it stands, which in turn comes from the Norman 'baillie' meaning fortified place, is built on the site of what was Newgate Prison. This was the jail for the entire City of London and the County of Middlesex, and was not the most pleasant of places to spend a night. Up to 16 people were crowded into each tiny cell, with just a few ventilation holes opening out onto the streets above. Yuk! It was so unpopular that in 1381 the prison was destroyed by Watt Tyler during the Peasants' Revolt. Then it was burnt down in the Great Fire of London, and finally, during the Gordon Riots in 1780, the prison was destroyed again.

Today, when the courts are in session members of the public can view the proceedings for free. But be warned: no mobile phones, cameras, recording equipment, radios, bags, packages, food, drink or children under 14 can be taken into the courts and there are no facilities for property to be left anywhere.

So stroll on down to the Old Bailey and watch the English legal system in action.

And afterwards. . . There are two interesting pubs linked with the notorious Newgate Prison. Firstly there's the Magpie and Stump (hmmm. . . nice), which is across the road from the Old Bailey. The original pub faced directly towards the gallows of Newgate Prison, and 'execution breakfasts' were a speciality of the house. There is nothing left of the original pub and the modern one that replaces is up an alleyway called Bishop's Court. Then there's the Viaduct Tavern, built in 1869. There is one permanent resident - a ghost called Fred, and two original cells from the prison. If you speak nicely to the landlord he may take you on a tour!

The Old Operating Theatre, Museum & Herb Garret

CAN YOU STILL HEAR THE SCREAMING?

9a St Thomas's Street, London, SE1 9RY
Telephone: 020 7955 4791
Underground: London Bridge
Admission: £3.75 Concessions: £2.75 Children: £2.25 Family Ticket: £9
Length of time required for visit: 50 mins – 1 hour
Open: 10:30am – 5:00pm Daily
Web site: www.thegarret.org.uk

Directions

Exit London Bridge station by the taxi ranks. Turn right towards Borough High Street. When you reach the High Street, turn left. The next road down is St. Thomas's Street – turn left here and the Old Operating Theatre is about 200 yards on your left.

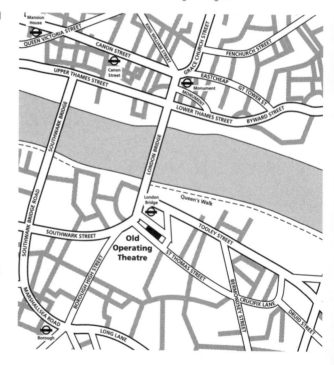

Amputations, blood-letting, trepanning (drilling holes in the skull). . . yes, it all went on here – with no anaesthetic! This is the site of Britain's oldest operating theatre and operations were performed here during the 1800s – before anaesthetic was invented and before anyone thought that keeping the place clean might be a good idea.

The theatre itself is actually in the roof space of the church and, combined with the museum and the herb garret, is one of London's most intriguing and unusual attractions. It offers a chilling (and gory) insight into the development of surgery and medical practices throughout the 1800s.

Try it out for yourself. Lie down on the original wooden operating table and imagine the scene. You're in for an amputation, fully conscious and your only crumb of comfort is a blindfold. If the shock doesn't kill you, the loss of blood or an infection probably will.

Why is the operating theatre in such a strange location? Well, the church was once part of St. Thomas's Hospital which was largely demolished in 1862 when it was relocated to Lambeth. The operating theatre was constructed in the roof space of the church so that the screams didn't distress the patients in the hospital wards.

The museum exhibits many surgical instruments from the 1800s. Some of these are unbelievably gruesome and, even as late as the mid-1800s, many were very similar to those used in Roman times.

If all this isn't enough, you can attend lectures here and find out even more!

And afterwards. . . The George Inn is highly recommended. Now owned by the National Trust, this is London's only surviving 16th Century galleried coaching inn and it can be found at George Inn Yard, signposted from Borough High Street.

There is a large courtyard which is very pleasant on a warm day but the pub can get very busy during summer.

OXO Tower and Gabriel's Wharf

VEGETARIANS WELCOME!

South Bank, SE1 9BH
Telephone: 020 7401 2255
Underground: Southwark, Blackfriars, Waterloo
Admission: Free
Length of time required for visit: 1 hour
Open: Shops and studios - Tue-Sun 11am-6pm, Restaurants and bars - Daily until late
Web site: www.oxotower.co.uk or www.gabrielswharf.co.uk

Directions
From Southwark underground take the Blackfriars Road exit. Turn left down Blackfriars Road towards the river. Before the bridge take the steps down to join the riverside walk known as Queen's Walk. The OXO Tower and Gabriel's Wharf are on the left. From Blackfriars underground walk across Blackfriars Bridge to the South Bank and join Queen's Walk as before.

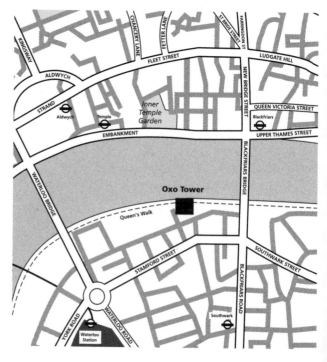

In the 1920's the Stamford Wharf was acquired by the Liebig Extract of Meat Company (what a mouthful, no wonder they shortened it to OXO!), and became a beef processing factory. Being sited on the river meant that the meat could be transported down the Thames on barges, and then hoisted directly into the factory. In 1928 the OXO Tower was built and became infamous for advertising the well-known stock cube by the letters being built into the tower windows and then lit up at night - defying the then ban on outdoor advertising.

Today the OXO Tower Wharf (as it is now known) is a much more pleasant location to visit. There are small designer shops and studios, galleries, exhibitions, and restaurants including the famous Harvey Nichols Oxo Tower restaurant. However best of all it is free to visit everything (unless of course you eat or buy anything!) including the rooftop viewing gallery, which gives great views across the river to St. Paul's Cathedral and the City.

Next door there is Gabriel's Wharf which has a variety of restaurants and bars, and more arts and crafts shops than you could shake a rain-stick at.

And afterwards. . . Try Doggett's pub just by Blackfriars Bridge. This was originally known as Doggett's Coat and Badge, and is named after the scarlet coat and badge which is awarded to the winner of a single skulls race for apprentice watermen or boatmen. It is the oldest annually contested event in the British sporting calendar and was instigated in 1716 by Thomas Doggett an Irish theatre manager/actor, who was very grateful to the boatmen who used to row him and other wealthy passengers across the river.

Prince Henry's Room

PLASTERED IN THE 17TH CENTURY!

Pepys' Chambers, 17 Fleet Street, London, EC4Y 1AA
Telephone: 020 7936 4004
Underground: Chancery Lane
Admission: Free
Length of time required for visit: 40 – 50 mins
Open: 11am-2pm Monday – Saturday
Web site: none

Directions
From Chancery
Lane tube take
the Chancery Lane
exit. Turn left into
Chancery Lane
and follow it down
to Fleet Street.
Prince Henry's
Room is opposite
where Chancery
Lane meets Fleet
Street.

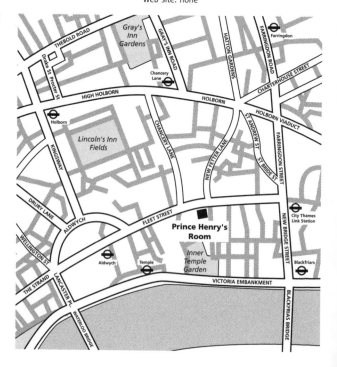

The Great Fire of London tried and failed, the World War Two blitz had a go and the heavy London traffic has been trying for years but amazingly enough Prince Henry's Room is still standing! Yes, against the odds, this timber framed building has survived here on Fleet Street since 1515.

Not only that but the original Jacobean plaster ceiling is still intact along with an intricate Jacobean oak panelled wall.

All the more amazing when you also take into account the fact that the building has been used for all kinds of other purposes since Prince Henry's days. At one point the building was taken over by 'Old Mother Salmon's Waxworks' – which received a mention in Dickens' *The Old Curiosity Shop*.

And Prince Henry? Sadly, longevity and survival are not words that we can associate with the Prince himself. He was the son of King James I and moved here in 1610 when he became Prince of Wales at the age of 16. Unfortunately, he died of typhoid only two years later.

The room itself is now home to a small exhibition of Samuel Pepys memorabilia. Pepys was born in Salisbury Court just off Fleet Street – only 200 yards away – and he is famous for his diaries that recorded his life and times in London during the 1660s. However, you might be surprised to learn that Pepys achieved a great deal more in his life – Member of Parliament, Master of Trinity House, President of the Royal Society – to name a few.

So, although it's only small, here we have two attractions in one! The unique delights of Price Henry's Room combined with a small Pepys-show. . .

And afterwards. . . Turn right on leaving Prince Henry's Room and just a few doors away you'll find the distinctive Olde Cock Tavern. This historic pub also survived the Great Fire and Pepys himself mentions drinking here in his diary. Alternatively, a few doors further along Fleet Street you'll find The Tipperary - this is the oldest Irish pub in London and there is an account of its fascinating history at the front of the pub.

Royal Academy of Arts

The Royal Academy of Arts

WHERE DAMIEN HIRST MEETS MONET. . .

Burlington House, Piccadilly, London, W1J 0BD
Telephone: 020 7300 5959
Underground: Green Park, Piccadilly Circus
Admission: £7.00 approx but varies according to exhibition
Concessions: £6.00 approx but varies according to exhibition
Length of time required for visit: 50mins – 1 hour
Open: 10am – 6pm daily (until 10pm Fridays)
Web site: www.royalacademy.org.uk

Directions
From Green Park and Piccadilly Circus tubes , take the Piccadilly north side exit. At street level head left from Green Park, from Piccadilly Circus head right..

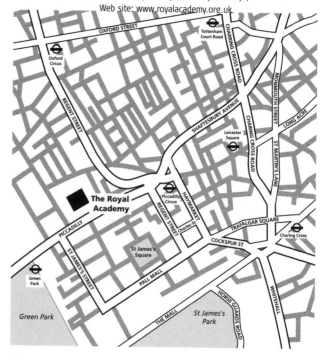

Well, one million customers a year can't be wrong! Here we have one of the world's most popular art galleries – earning a regular place in London's top ten attractions for paying visitors. Stunning exhibitions, a mixture of old and new, paintings, sculptures, contemporary artists, past masters. . . they're all here.

So, how does it all work? Well, there is a permanent collection but mainly we are talking about exhibitions – and hugely successful and popular ones at that.

To start with, there is the Summer Exhibition. In fact, there has been a Summer Exhibition at the RA every single year since 1769! The aim is to show contemporary art and it is open to all artists – it has now become the largest open contemporary art exhibition in the world. The Summer Exhibition provides an intriguing mix of work by the very eminent Royal Academicians, work by invited artists and also Open Submissions. Any artist can submit work, so an emerging artist could potentially end up hanging with the likes of David Hockney, Damien Hirst or Tracey Emin.

And, many of the works in the Summer Exhibition are for sale – so don't forget your credit card!

Then there are the loan exhibitions which usually last for about four months at a time. The most successful in recent times – in fact one of the most successful art exhibitions of all time – was 'Monet in the 20th Century' which attracted 800,000 visitors. The latest and forthcoming exhibitions are usually very well publicised. Prices vary according to the exhibitions and for some of the more popular ones it is sometimes necessary to book.

And afterwards. . . Even if your credit card's taken a spanking, you'll surely have a few quid left for a pint or two at the small and cosy Chequers Tavern in Duke Street – which is opposite the front of the RA and the pub can be found on the left about 75 yards along. Originally the Masons Arms, this pub was one of the first buildings erected after the Great Fire of London 1666 – a more detailed history is on display inside.

The Royal College *of* Surgeons *of* England

The Royal College of Surgeons of England

AT THE CUTTING EDGE. . .

35-43 Lincoln's Inn Fields, WC2A 3PE
Telephone: 020 7869 6560
Underground: Holborn
Admission: Free
Length of time required for visit: 1 hour
Open: 10am-5pm Monday-Friday, closed weekends and Bank Holidays
Web site: www.rceng.ac.uk/museums

Directions
From Holborn tube, exit onto Kingsway and turn left. Keep going until you meet Sardinia Street and turn left down here. Bear to the right with Lincoln's Inn Fields on your left. The museum is housed in a grand building on your right, but it has only a small plaque on the gate to indicate where it is.

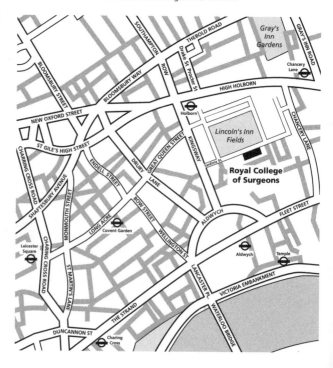

In 1540 the Company of Barber Surgeons was founded. Later, in 1745, the surgeons split up from the hairdressers and formed a separate company. This museum is the work of the father figure of scientific surgery, John Hunter (1728-1793), and is arranged as he originally set it out over 200 years ago. Visiting here is like being in a time warp - you get the feeling that Burke and Hare could appear from behind the cabinets at any moment.

Now this museum is not for the squeamish. On show here is wall to wall pickled everything - I mean you name it and it'll probably be in a jar here somewhere - from brains to bats' wings. After all, there are 3,500 specimens on the ground floor alone, and if you've got time another 2,500 upstairs.

Then there is always the skeleton of Charles Byrne, the 'Irish Giant', to measure yourself up against. Or if that's a bit tame, then try coming face to face with a murderer or two. The Company of Surgeons were allowed to publicly dissect executed criminals, but they also used bodies provided by grave robbers, until this was outlawed in 1832.

In addition to the Hunterian Museum there is also the Odontological Museum – that's teeth and skulls to you and me – and there's more in here to wonder at. So if you're in the mood for something different, then this bizarre collection is definitely worth a visit.

And afterwards. . . Enjoy a pint and a pickled egg at the Ship Tavern. Exit the Museum, turn left and cross over to the green area of Lincoln's Inn Fields, skirt around the edge of this. The Ship Tavern is in a narrow alleyway where Gate Street meets Little Turnstile and you should be able to see it straight ahead. Established in 1549 it has a very interesting past.

ROYAL OPERA HOUSE
COVENT GARDEN

The Royal Opera House - Backstage Tour

GO BEHIND THE IRON CURTAIN. . .

Covent Garden, WC2E 9DD
Telephone: 020 7304 4000
Underground: Covent Garden
Admission: £8.00   Concessions: £7.00
Length of time required for visit: 1¼ hours
Open: Tours run at 10.30am, 12.30 and 2.30pm but booking is essential
Web site: www.royaloperahouse.org

Directions
From Covent
Garden
underground turn
right down James
Street towards the
central market of
Covent Garden,
then skirt left
around the central
market area. The
entrance to the
Royal Opera House
linkway is on your
left.

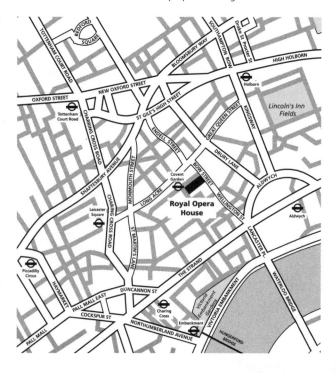

Two disastrous fires, two world wars, and the bustling fruit and vegetable market on its doorstep – the Royal Opera House has survived much in its history.

Confused as to why the Royal Opera House also houses the Royal Ballet? And how the opera productions can possibly run alongside the ballet productions? What does a 'touch-up artist' really do for a living? And why were 'the stalls' called the stalls? Well, this guided backstage tour explains all. It also describes the colourful past of the theatre and its audiences, and takes you behind the scenes in a fascinating tour.

Sit on those plush velvet seats and imagine you're in for a night at the opera. Performances have been going on hereabouts since John Rich built the first theatre in 1732. However, it is the version that was built in 1858 that has been completely refurbished. Opera audiences may have a reputation for being reserved, but they are certainly not afraid to show their opinions - just ask the cat that got thrown down from the gallery during one performance. Sitting in the stalls and looking up you will see that it is a jolly long way down!

The auditorium is now part of a 2.5 acre site. Sounds massive doesn't it - most of this is taken up with the stage and backstage mechanisms, but there are the full-size rehearsal stages, the ballet studios and the onsite props and costume departments to fit in.

So brush up on your arias and try out the tour of the Royal Opera House.

And afterwards. . . Take a stroll around the block to the Kemble's Head – just turn left on exiting the front of the opera house. This corner pub where Bow Street meets Long Acre celebrates John Philip Kemble a famous Shakespearean actor and manager of the Drury Lane and Covent Garden Theatres. But be on your best behaviour as Bow Street police station is just across the road, where the 'Bow Street Runners' formed the first police force in Britain in 1750.

Directions

From St. Paul's underground, take exit 1 and turn left at the top of the steps along Newgate Street. Turn right down Giltspur Street at the main traffic lights. St. Barts is about 100 yards on your right, but continue on until you meet the north wing entrance and walk under the arch. Continue past the church and the museum is on your left. From the Barbican underground, turn right down Long Lane heading towards Smithfield market, then with the market on your right, turn left, and St. Barts Hospital is on your left. Turn left into the north entrance and follow instructions as before.

St Bartholomew's Hospital Museum

HOSPITALITY AT ITS BEST

West Smithfield, EC1A 7BE
Telephone: 020 7601 8152
Underground: St. Paul's, Barbican
Admission: Free
Length of time required for visit: 40 minutes
Open: Tue-Fri 10am-4pm
Web site: www.brlcf.org.uk

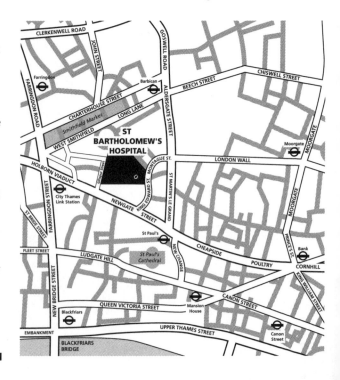

Back in the days of 1123, Smithfield was a smooth field, a patch of dry ground amidst a very wet, marshy and smelly backwater of London. It had the added attraction of being a popular place to hang thieves. That was until Rahere, (previously a fulltime party animal in the court of Henry I, but then reformed into a monk and all-round good guy) had a vision whilst sick on a pilgrimage to Rome. In return for regaining his health he vowed to a build a hospital that would help the poorest and neediest. He chose Smithfield as the place, and St. Bartholomew's Hospital was born.

Here at the museum you get a chance to learn more about the fascinating history of St. Barts, how it has miraculously escaped closure many times including as recently as 1994, to become one of the oldest hospitals in the world. You can get nice and close to some pretty gruesome surgical instruments and even peruse a book of artistic drawings of ailments and diseases (very useful in the days before cameras and films). Best you don't have lunch first!

So to find out what a 'bougie' did, or what a set of 18th century 'lunatic restrainers' looked like, then come and enjoy true hospitality at St. Barts Museum.

And afterwards. . . Try the Bishop's Finger which is across the other side of the gardens, and can be seen from the north wing entrance of the hospital. Despite its odd name it has no historical connection to the hospital.

St Paul's Cathedral

St Paul's Cathedral

NOT FOR THE FAINT-HEARTED. . .

Ludgate Hill, EC4M 8AD
Telephone: 020 7236 4128
Underground: St. Paul's, Mansion House
Admission: £6.00 Concessions: £5.00
Length of time required for visit: 50 mins – 1 hour
Open: 8.30am-4pm Mon-Sat
Web site: www.stpauls.co.uk

Directions
Take exit 2 from
St. Paul's tube
station and you
are at the back of
the cathedral. Exit
from Mansion
House
underground and
turn left along
Cannon Street. St.
Paul's is about
400 yards ahead.

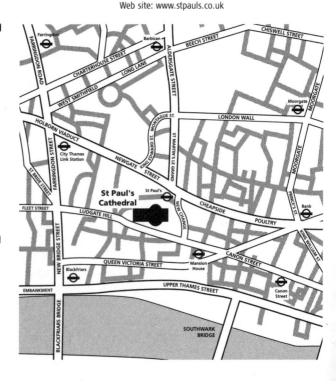

September 1666 and the 3rd largest church in Europe has just been razed to the ground in the Great Fire of London. St Paul's Cathedral had an unlucky start. Its forerunners, a wooden Saxon church, which burnt down and was rebuilt many times, and the fabulous gothic Norman cathedral with the tallest spire ever built in England, was struck by lightning twice and was finally destroyed beyond repair in the Great Fire of 1666. It's a wonder Sir Christopher Wren's replacement has survived the ravages of Civil War, the Industrial Revolution, two World Wars and all that the pigeons of London can throw at it! But it has.

And afterwards. . . Try the Bell, Book and Candle which is straight down Ludgate Hill from the main exit of St Paul's.

The architect Sir Christopher Wren was chosen to design and oversee the rebuilding of St. Paul's in 1669. Deadlines weren't quite so demanding in those days, and a mere 35 years later the Cathedral was complete. Mind you, when you get inside and see how overwhelmingly grand and ornate the Cathedral is, you can appreciate why it took so long.

A good overall view may be obtained from the Whispering Gallery only 259 shallow steps to reach this! Try out the 'Whisper Test', where a whisper made against one side of the circular wall can be heard on the opposite side, 42 metres away.

If you are fit and able bodied, and definitely don't suffer from vertigo, pass through base camp (the Whispering Gallery) and make the ascent of 530 steps to the 'Golden Gallery' at the top. You are now 280 feet above ground level. Take a deep breath and then admire the fantastic panorama of London. Interestingly there are 543 steps to get your breath back on the way down!

The crypt is also recommended. Here are the resting places of former celebrities, such as the Duke of Wellington and Nelson. Take time out to read some great epitaphs.

Shakespeare's Globe Theatre – Exhibition Tour

ARE YOU A BUDDING THESPIAN?
New Globe Walk, SE1 9DT
Telephone: Box Office 020 7902 1500
Underground: Southwark, Blackfriars
Admission: £8.00 (guided tour) £5.00 (virtual tour)
Concessions: £6.50, £4.00
Length of time required for visit: 1 hour
Open: Oct-Apr 10am-5pm daily. May-Sep 9am-noon, exhibition and guided tour of the theatre. 1.00-4pm, exhibition and 'virtual tour' of the theatre
Web site: www.shakespeares-globe.org

Directions
From Southwark underground take the Blackfriars Road exit. Cross Blackfriars Road at the traffic lights and walk along Union Street. Turn left down Great Suffolk Street and cross Southwark Street. Skirt round the Tate Modern and join Queen's Walk with the river on your left. The Globe is just past the Millennium Bridge. From Blackfriars underground walk across Blackfriars Bridge to the South Bank and then along Queen's Walk as before.

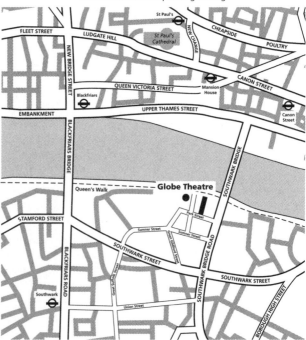

To be, or not to be: that is the question. *Hamlet*
Cry 'God for Harry! England and Saint George!' *Henry V*
Double, double toil and trouble; Fire burn and cauldron bubble.
Macbeth
If music be the food of love, play on. *Twelfth Night*

Imagine yourself on the stage of Shakespeare's Globe Theatre reciting these immortal lines. Well, the exhibition tour could be the nearest you'll get to it. Here you can touch the stage and imagine you're back in Shakespeare's time – hazelnut shells and straw scattered beneath your feet, the audience full of unsavoury characters - prostitutes, gamblers, drunken revellers, even perhaps royalty. If you fluff your lines, only the height of the stage saves you from a potentially violent mobbing.

From inside the theatre you can admire the beautiful oak beams, and wonder at how 6,000 wooden pegs hold the whole thing together, along with some sand, slaked lime and animal hair!

Reconstruction of this theatre was the dream of the actor and director Sam Wanamaker. In 1949 he tried to find the site of the original Globe Theatre, but all he found was a plaque on the side of a disused brewery! Nearly 50 years later the reconstructed Globe opened for its first performance. The exhibition pays tribute to Sam Wanamaker and how his dream became reality. It gives a real insight as to what Southwark was like in Shakespeare's day. But you can also listen to your favourite actors reciting your favourite soliloquies and even have a go at editing Hamlet. So pop along to the exhibition and discover the thespian inside you.

And afterwards. . . Just up the river towards Southwark Bridge is the historic Anchor at Bankside. A pub has existed on this site for over 800 years. In fact Samuel Pepys watched the Great Fire of London from this very spot in 1666. You, too, can admire a fine view of the City (hopefully not in flames) from the many outside tables.

Shakespeare's Globe Theatre - A Performance

A FROLICKING GOOD TIME. . .

21 New Globe Walk, SE1 9DT

Telephone: Box Office 020 7401 9919

Underground: Southwark, Blackfriars

Admission: Standing £5.00 Seated £10.00-£27.00

Concessions: Senior citizens, NUS, disabled & 1 companion, children under 16.

No concessions on standing tickets.

Length of time required for visit: Duration of play - normally 3 hours

Open: May to September afternoon and evening performances

Web site: www.shakespeares-globe.org

Directions

From Southwark underground take the Blackfriars Road exit. Cross Blackfriars Road at the traffic lights and walk along Union Street. Turn left down Great Suffolk Street and cross Southwark Street. Skirt round the Tate Modern and join the Queen's Walk with the river on your left. The Globe is just past the Millennium Bridge. From Blackfriars underground walk across Blackfriars Bridge to the South Bank and then along Queen's Walk as before.

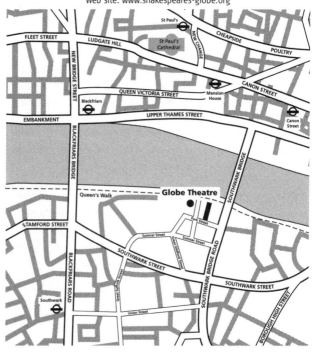

Do you fancy standing on your feet for 3 hours, exposed to the elements, watching a Shakespeare play and paying for the pleasure? If not, then think again, a fiver could not be more well spent, anywhere in the country.

The plays are performed from May to September, when hopefully the English weather is at its kindest. You will probably need to book in advance, although tickets can often be obtained on the day. If you choose the £5 standing ticket you will become what is officially termed a 'groundling'. This allows you to stand anywhere in the pit in front of the stage. It also means that if you don't like your view, you can move about until you do, or even more surprisingly pop outside and get a coffee and a snack mid-performance.

This is how Shakespeare wrote the plays to be performed, in front of an audience that is part of the proceedings. The interaction between the groundlings and the players can have an influence on the success of the performance, and so the humorous parts are normally played up. In fact a bit of light banter is positively encouraged, but don't expect to be dragged up onto the stage in pop concert style.

The three hours simply fly by. One warning though – wrap up warm and keep your waterproofs handy, if not for the weather, you never know what the actors might throw at you! So if you want to feel part of a unique performance, head on down to the Globe.

And afterwards. . . Just up the river towards Southwark Bridge is the historic Anchor at Bankside. A pub has existed on this site for over 800 years. In fact Samuel Pepys watched the Great Fire of London from this very spot in 1666. You, too, can admire a fine view of the City (hopefully not in flames) from the many outside tables.

THE
SHERLOCK
HOLMES
MUSEUM

The Sherlock Holmes Museum

DEAR MR HOLMES. . .

221b Baker Street, London, NW1 6XE
Telephone: 020 7935 8866
Underground: Baker Street
Admission: £6.00 Children under 16: £4.00
Length of time required for visit: 50mins
Open: 9:30am-6pm daily
Web site: www.sherlock-holmes.co.uk

Directions
From Baker Street tube take the Baker Street north exit and turn right at street level. The museum is about 75 yards away on the other side of the road. Incidentally, if you exit via the front of the station, you will usually find Sherlock himself handing out his 'Consulting Detective' business cards – with directions to the museum on the back.

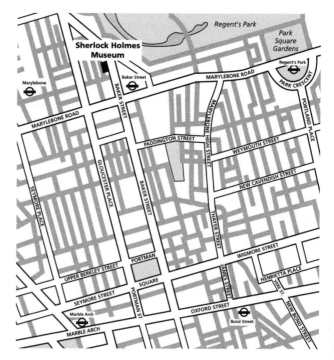

Victorian pea-soupers, horse-drawn carriages, cobblestones, gaslight. . . and then. . . Professor Moriarty with Holmes and Watson in hot pursuit. Yes – the legend of Sherlock Holmes is celebrated in considerable style here at 221b Baker Street.

Now, you won't need Holmes's famous deductive powers to work out that this may not exactly be 221b and even the most bumbling of Watson's amongst you will be aware that our two heroes, errr. . . didn't actually exist at all – but never mind all that! What's certain is that there is more Sherlock memorabilia here than you can puff your pipe smoke at. Fans of Holmes and Conan Doyle, crime fiction buffs and even just the mildly curious will love it.

The house that the museum is based in was actually a Holmes-style lodging house in Victorian times and it is furnished just how you would expect it to be if Holmes and Watson had lived here. There are exhibitions of scenes and characters from the stories along with many of the objects and trappings from Conan Doyle's world of Holmes and Watson.

Do you have a real-life mystery of your own that needs solving? Well, why not write to the man himself and ask for an opinion – hundreds of people actually write to the great detective and a selection of these letters can be found at the Museum.

And afterwards. . . The Volunteer can be found just a few doors away at number 245. Not much Holmes-related memorabilia here but watch out for the ghost that reputedly haunts the cellar!

Sir John Soane's Museum

A REAL-LIFE ALADDIN'S CAVE. . . TO EDUCATE AND INSPIRE

13 Lincoln's Inn Fields, London, WC2A 3BP
Telephone: 020 7405 2107
Underground: Holborn
Admission: Free, but £3 for the Saturday museum tour at 2.30pm
All goups must book in advance and a donation of £25 is requested
Length of time required for visit: 50mins – 1 hour
Open: 10am – 5pm Tuesday - Saturday Closed Bank Holidays
Web site: www.soane.org

Directions
From Holborn tube, exit onto Kingsway and turn left. After about 50 yards, turn left into Remnant Street – this short street runs into Lincoln's Inn Fields and the museum is then about 50 yards on the left.

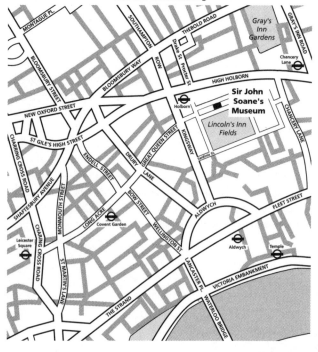

Now, not many people open up their own house as a museum but that's exactly what Sir John Soane did in 1833 – while he was still living there! And not only that, he obtained an Act of Parliament to ensure that the house and collection would be preserved and that free access would be allowed for the public and, of course, students in architecture, painting and sculpture.

Sir John Soane was one of England's greatest architects. He progressed from being a building site labourer at the age of 15 to architect to the Bank of England and, later, Professor of Architecture at the Royal Academy. But he was also a collector and, along the way, he accumulated a vast array of paintings, books, statues, objects Roman, artefacts Egyptian and countless other things of interest from all over the world.

So how did he find room for everything given the limited space available? After all, this was also his home! Well, the design and layout of the house/museum and the way that just about every available nook and cranny has been utilised really has to be seen to be believed. Make sure you pick up the pamphlet titled 'A Short Description' on your way in – this gives you the route through the house that was recommended by Soane himself.

Also, don't miss the hidden secrets of the Picture Room! There are walls within walls with a surprise at the end bathed in yellow light. A member of staff should be available to give you a full demonstration of how this brilliantly designed room works.

And afterwards. . . The Ship Tavern can be found in a narrow alleyway (Gate Street) – you can see it when you cross between Remnant Street and Lincoln's Inn Fields. Established in 1549, this pub has plenty of history. Alternatively, there is the Shakespeare's Head at 64-68 Kinsgway, near Holborn tube.

SOMERSET HOUSE

Somerset House

A MIXED BAG. . .

Somerset House, Strand WC2R
Telephone: 020 7845 4600
Underground: Temple, Covent Garden
Admission: Free into Somerset House, prices vary for the galleries
Length of time required for visit: 1 hour upwards
Open: 10am-6pm daily, including Bank Holidays
Web site: www.somerset-house.org.uk

Directions
From Temple underground, exit onto the Victoria embankment and head towards Waterloo Bridge - the Embankment entrance to Somerset House is on your right. From Covent Garden underground, turn right down Long Acre, then turn right along Bow Street. Carry straight on. You are now on Wellington Street. Keep going until you meet the Strand, cross over at the traffic lights and turn left - the Strand entrance to Somerset House is on your right.

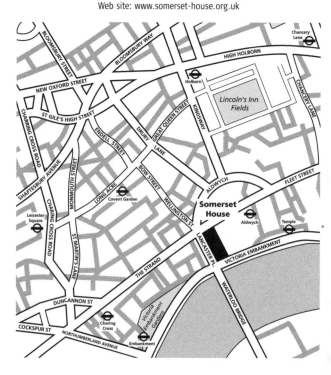

The River Terrace, the Great Arch, the King's Barge House, the Nelson Stair, the Stamp Stair, the Seaman's Waiting Hall, the Dead House, the Fountain Court - not to mention shed loads of history to keep you busy here.

Why not have tea on the River Terrace overlooking the Thames, marvel at the Great Arch and the King's Barge House, ponder at Nelson's Stair (why?), wonder at the Stamp Stairs (how?), or just relax in the Seaman's Waiting Hall? You can walk along the lightwells to the Dead House - if you can find it, or admire the Fountain Court, but it's probably best to get a guided tour (every Thursday and Saturday 1.30pm and 3.45pm and costs £2.75), to appreciate all these things to the full.

The first Somerset House was a Tudor palace built in 1547 by Edward Seymour, known as 'Protector Somerset'. But he soon fell out of favour and was executed. Hmmm! Royalty then requisitioned the building for their own purposes and it was used for special occasions and even as a dowager's house. Not a bad little number. However in the 18th century the building was very neglected and in 1775 Sir William Chambers was given the task of rebuilding the palace as a purpose-built government building.

There are also various art collections to be enjoyed in the Courtauld Institute gallery, Gilbert Collection and Hermitage Rooms (these aren't free). So hit the Strand and see what's on at Somerset House, but be warned, The Inland Revenue is still in residence!

And afterwards. . . Pop down to the Wellington pub, which is towards Covent Garden underground, or try the Lyceum Tavern almost next door. This is a typical English pub with dark wood panelling and hunting prints everywhere.

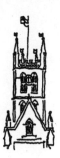

Southwark Cathedral

THE OLDEST GOTHIC BUILDING IN LONDON

Montague Close, SE1 9DA
Telephone: 020 7367 6700
Underground: London Bridge, Monument
Admission: Cathedral by donation - suggested £2 per person, Visitor Centre £3.00
Concession: Visitor Centre £2.50
Length of time required for visit: Cathedral 1 hour. Visitor Centre 30 mins
Open: 10am-6pm daily
Web site: www.dswark.org/cathedral

Directions
From London
Bridge tube
station, take
either the Duke
Street Hill exit or
the Tooley Street
exit. Turn left and
the cathedral is on
the other side of
the road. From
Monument, cross
London Bridge on
the right hand
side and descend
the steps at the
end of the bridge
to access the
Cathedral via the
Millennium
Courtyard.

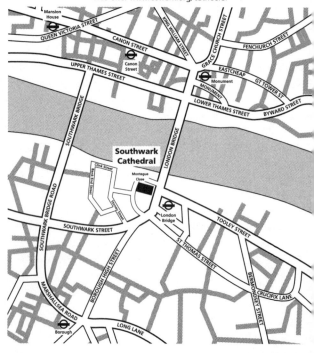

852AD and St. Swithun, Bishop of Winchester, is planning to set up a college of priests on the site that is now occupied by Southwark Cathedral. He probably did not realise it at the time but he was laying the foundations for a place of worship that would witness over one thousand years of history.

Following on from St. Swithun, a basic history of Southwark Cathedral is as follows:- 1106 - the Norman priory church of St. Mary Overie was built; 1212 – the church was re-built as a magnificent Gothic structure after the Southwark Fire; 1539 – became the parish church of St. Saviour; 1905 – the church became Southwark Cathedral.

Quite clearly, therefore, Southwark Cathedral has an intriguing and varied history: the Norman Conquest, Richard II, the Reformation, the Elizabethan era, Victorian England, the Industrial Revolution – all the way through to its modern-day role in the diocese of Southwark.

If all that wasn't enough, Nelson Mandela arrived in April 2001 to open a £10 million pound development consisting of a new Visitor Centre, refectory, library, shop and the Millennium Courtyard.

The Visitor Centre provides a high-tech audio-visual experience themed on views of London. The inspiration for this is the 'The Long View of London' – as drawn from the Cathedral tower in 1638 by Wenceslas Hollar. In the centre itself, aspects of local history are explained and a mini-cinema has a continuously showing film which deals with the history of Southwark from Roman times onwards.

Also on display, are locally found artefacts – including a pair of bone ice-skates that were used for skating on the Thames during the Frost Fairs in the 1600s!

And afterwards. . . The Cathedral Refectory operated by Digby Trout Restaurant offers food and drink and on a nice day you can sit outside in the Millennium Courtyard. If you fancy something a little stronger, immediately next door to the courtyard (London Bridge side) is a pub called the MudLark.

Tate Modern

MORE THAN A PILE OF BRICKS. . .

Bankside, SE1 9TG
Telephone: 020 7887 8008
Underground: Southwark, Blackfriars
Admission: Gallery is free but donations welcome, Exhibitions - Prices vary
Length of time required for visit: 1 hour upwards
Open: Sun-Thu 10am-6pm, Fri,Sat 10am-10pm
Web site: www.tate.org.uk

Directions
From Southwark underground take the Blackfriars Road exit. Cross Blackfriars Road at the traffic lights and walk along Union Street. Turn left down Great Suffolk Street and cross Southwark Street. Ahead is the back of Tate Modern. From Blackfriars walk across Blackfriars Bridge to the South Bank and walk down the steps to join the Queen's Walk with the river on your left. Tate Modern is just before the Millennium Bridge.

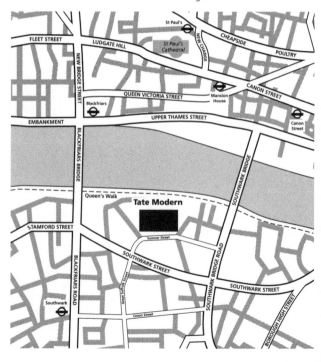

Dali, Picasso, Matisse, Rothko, Warhol and Emin – they're all here. But where's here?

Well, in 1947 a huge industrial building began its life on the south bank, 500 feet long (that's longer than a full-size football pitch) with a 325-feet high chimney. This was a state-of-the-art oil fired power station to supply post-war London's ever increasing demands. It took 16 years to build and its working life lasted just a little longer - 18 years. It then lay unused and unloved for another 16 years with everyone wondering what to do with the monstrosity.

Then in 2000, with a little help from the Swiss architects Herzog and de Meuron, along with a few builders, the former power station was transformed into a new home for the Tate's modern art collection. No longer hidden away in storage, everything is unpacked and on show here, in the perfect surroundings for 20th century pieces.

Perhaps you've always wondered what makes a pile of bricks art? Or you've always wanted to see Rodin's 'The Kiss' sitting next to a Jackson Pollock! Well now's your chance and it's all free. There are seminars and workshops, and great views of the city from the 4th floor restaurant and the galleries, so trot on down to Tate Modern and let your imagination run away with you.

And afterwards. . . The Founders Arms is an octagonal pub right outside Tate Modern and directly on the riverside walkway. It was built in 1979 on the site of the foundry where the bells for St. Paul's Cathedral were cast, and offers great views of St. Paul's and the 'Millennium bridge'!

The Theatre Museum

GET A BACKSTAGE PASS. . .

Russell Street, WC2E 7PR
Telephone: 020 7943 4700
Underground: Covent Garden
Admission: Free for individuals. For group prices call 020 7943 4806
Length of time required for visit: 1 hour
Open: Tuesday-Sunday 10am-6pm, closed Bank Holidays
Web site: www.theatremuseum.org

Directions
From Covent
Garden
underground turn
right down James
Street towards the
central market of
Covent Garden,
then skirt left
around the busy
market area until
you meet Russell
Street. Turn left
down Russell
Street and the
Theatre Museum
is on your right.

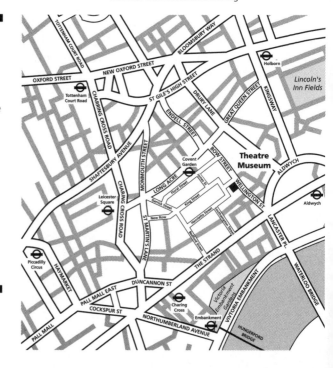

The year is 1613, and there's something going down in Southwark! A few friends are off to see Shakespeare's latest blockbuster *Henry V* . Now this is to be a serious session of fun - firstly there's the trek over to Southwark across London Bridge, then perhaps a quick bath and a bit of the other in one of the stew-houses on the way to the Globe. The performance itself will probably last about six hours, so that just leaves time for a spot of entertainment in one of the bear-baiting pits on the way home. Phew, they knew how to party in the early 1600s.

However, life in theatre-world did not always go strictly to plan! For instance the first Globe Theatre actually burnt down, when a cannon set fire to the thatched roof during a performance of *Henry V*. But a second Globe was soon erected and theatres have been changing ever since.

The Theatre Museum, which is housed in the old Flower Market building of Covent Garden, celebrates the history of the stage, its playwrights, and the actors and actresses during the last 400 years. There are models of the theatres, actual costumes, billboards, and marionettes, as well as temporary exhibitions, but to find out more about this fascinating heritage, join one of the tours around the museum galleries. Or be a model for the make-up demonstration and spend the rest of the day scaring people with a realistic flesh wound! You can also try on costumes and walk on stage, join in various workshops, or operate the giant puppets, all for the entrance price.

And afterwards. . . Get legless in the Marquess of Angelsey! You'll be in very good company, as this pub honours Henry Paget, the Earl of Uxbridge *aka* the Marquess of Angelsey, who fought at the battle of Waterloo and lost a leg to one of the last shots of the day. Turn right on exiting the museum and the pub is across the road on the corner where Bow Street meets Russell Street.

95

Tower Bridge Experience

OPEN AND SHUT IN FIVE MINUTES

Tower Bridge, SE1 2UP
Telephone: 020 7403 3761
Underground: Tower Hill, London Bridge
Admission: £4.50 Concessions: £3.00 Family Ticket from £14
Length of time required for visit: 50mins
Open: 9.30am- 6.00pm all year but closed 24 & 25 December,
Web site: www.towerbridge.org.uk

Directions
Tower Bridge is
clearly signposted
from Tower Hill
tube station.

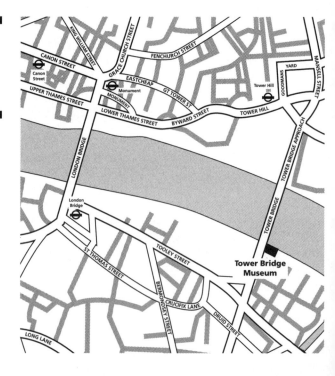

In August 1882, before Tower Bridge existed, a census revealed that over 100,000 pedestrians and 22,000 vehicles used London Bridge in a twenty-four hour period! So, it was decided that a new bridge across the Thames was required.

Step forward Horace Jones, the City Architect, with a proposal for a street-level bridge that could be raised to let ships through. What followed was hailed as a triumph for British engineering and the resultant Tower Bridge has since come to be recognised throughout the world as a symbol of London.

Not everyone realises that there is an award-winning attraction inside Tower Bridge. Here you will find the Tower Bridge Experience with shows, interactive computers, hands-on exhibitions – all dedicated to the history and upkeep of the bridge.

The most spectacular part of the Experience is the high-level walkways that span the Thames, 140 feet above it. The views, both upstream and downstream, are superb. Positioned along the walkways are photographs of how this part of the Thames looked in the early twentieth century – yes, there really was a Tower Beach!

The final part of the tour consists of an exploration of the Victorian steam engine rooms – complete with a hands-on gallery.

And afterwards. . . The tour finishes on the South bank of the river so a good place to quench your thirst is the Anchor Tap – just round the corner in Horselydown Lane. Head along Shad Thames and only about 20 yards from Tower Bridge you will find the site of the old Anchor Brewhouse – a wall plaque gives a brief history of the brewery and the brewing tradition of this area of the Thames. Turn right here and you will see the Anchor Tap. This ancient pub serves traditional English food, has a flower-filled beer garden and also 2 ghosts!

UNDERGROUND

London's Transport Museum

FROM HORSE-BUSES TO HOVER CARS. . .

Covent Garden Piazza, London, WC2E 7BB
Telephone: 020 7379 6344
Underground: Covent Garden
Admission: £5.95 Concessions: £4.50
Length of time required for visit: 1 hour
Open: 10am - 6pm daily (Fridays 11am – 6pm)
Web site: www.ltmuseum.co.uk

Directions
From Covent
Garden tube, turn
right into James
Street and take
the short walk to
the Piazza. When
you get there, go
round to the left –
the museum is
located in the
opposite corner.

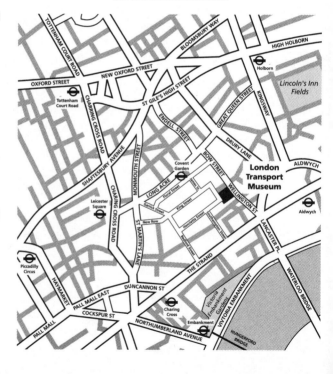

Well, the year is 1840 and you're travelling in a horse-bus but you need to get off. So, naturally, you tug at the straps attached to the driver's arms! Left or right depending on which side of the road you want! It might seem a little dangerous now but it's just one of the many weird and wonderful things that went on in the very early days of London transport.

Starting with the horse-bus. things progressed on to the horse-tram and horses were actually still being used for mass public transport until 1914. Then it was the turn of trams, trolley-buses and eventually the legendary red London motor bus.

During all this time, things were also happening below ground. The world's first underground railway, the Metropolitan line, opened in 1863 – with steam engines!

The full history of the development of the transport network in London is explained in clear and eye-catching style here at the award-winning London Transport Museum. Housed in the former Covent Garden Flower Market, there are plenty of real-life examples of just about everything associated with London transport.

You can climb on board original horse-buses, trams, early London motor-buses. Don't miss the Ladies-only carriage, dated 1900, from the Metropolitan Line with it's wood exterior and wooden floorboards. Also, you can have a go on the tube driver simulators.

And the future? Well, how about hover cars, bat gliders and perhaps even cable cars! These things and more are all speculated on in the *Welcome to the Future Exhibition* – which attempts to open your eyes to how London's transport systems might look in years to come.

And afterwards. . . Travelling back towards Covent Garden tube, you will find two suitable drinking establishments almost opposite each other and very close to the tube station: The Nags Head and the White Lion.

VINOPOLIS
CITY OF WINE

Vinopolis!

PUT YOUR DRINKING CAP ON!

No. 1 Bank End, SE1 9BU

Telephone: 0870 4444 777

Underground: London Bridge

Admission: £11.50 Concessions: Senior citizens: £10.50; child aged 5-15: £5; groups larger than 10: £10.50 (£1 discount each)

Length of time required for visit: 2 hours (last admission 2 hours before closing)

Open: 11am-6pm daily, Saturdays open until 8pm, Mondays open until 9pm, for December and Bank Holiday opening times ring 0870 241 4040

Web site: www.vinopolis.co.uk

Directions
Exit London Bridge underground station (Jubilee and Northern line) via the Borough High Street (west side) exit. At the top of the stairs walk straight on and then first right into Stoney Street. Then take the first turning left into Park Street and follow the road around until you meet the main Vinopolis entrance.

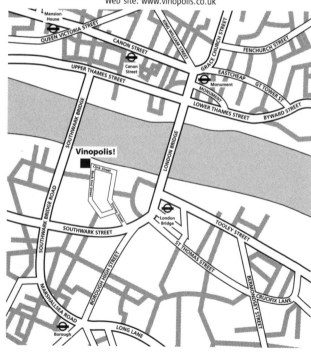

Chateau Lafite, Chateau La Tour, Chateau Neuf du Pape, or Dom Perignon – if these names are making your mouth water and you've a couple of hours to spare, then take time out to visit Vinopolis.

Here you can enjoy a wine-tasting demonstration (at a small additional charge) and then with a handy headset attached - known as your audio guide - you are ready to experience the world of wine.

The Vinopolis tour lets you meander through the wine regions of the world, taking in the cultures and history, but more importantly letting you sample the wines en route at the 'Tasting Tables'. You are automatically entitled to 5 samplings, but you can obtain another 5 for £2.50, or perhaps just bribe your friends to hand over their vouchers.

You can ride the Italian roads on a Vespa scooter (you won't get booked for drink/driving - promise), find out what smudge pots, disgorging and bin ends are, and what the locals get up to all in the name of making Port. There's a café half-way round if you need to pace yourself with a spot of lunch, so team up with some fellow wine-lovers and point yourselves in the direction of Vinopolis.

Note: Children are welcome at Vinopolis and will be offered fruit juices to taste as part of the tour. They're delicious too! There is also full access for guests with special needs.

And afterwards. . . Try sobering up by staggering around to the site of the remains of the Rose Theatre, built in 1587 and the forerunner to the Globe Theatre. Turn left on exiting Vinopolis and then first right into Park Street. There are AA signs clearly labelling the way and plenty of lampposts to hang onto if you're feeling a bit wobbly. Alternatively, enjoy the sights, sounds and smells, if you're up to it, of the famous Borough Market, by heading in the opposite direction.

The Wallace Collection

A FANTASTIC COLLECTION WITH A FRENCH CONNECTION. . .

Hertford House, Manchester Square, London, W1U 3BN
Telephone: 020 7563 9500
Underground: Bond Street
Admission: Free!
Length of time required for visit: 50 mins but several visits recommended
Open: 10am – 5pm Mon – Sat, 2pm – 5pm Sun
Web site: www.the-wallace-collection.org.uk

Directions
From Bond Street tube station, exit on to Oxford Street, cross over and head left towards Selfridges. Turn right immediately before Selfridges into Duke Street. Follow Duke Street until you reach Manchester Square – Hertford House is on the opposite side of the square.

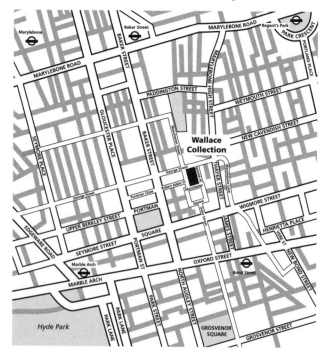

You might not believe this but, just a few minutes' walk from Selfridges, there is a huge mansion containing a vast privately-owned collection of priceless art-works and treasures gathered from all over the world. And how much does it cost to see it all? Nothing! Yes, you can browse round the Wallace Collection in Hertford House totally free of charge (although, please make a donation before you leave).

So, what's the story here then? Well, it's all down to the intriguing, complex and often scandalous history of the Seymour-Conways, Marquesses of Hertford. This is a tale of wealth, power, scandal, illegitimate offspring and debauchery – spanning four generations. Basically, the 2nd Marquess of Hertford acquired Hertford House in 1797. The 3rd and 4th Marquesses were avid connoisseurs and collectors of art and when the 4th Marquess died, he bequeathed the collection to his illegitimate son, Richard Wallace. The 4th Marquess and Richard Wallace both lived in Paris but in 1872, Wallace moved to London and continued to add to the Collection. After Sir Richard Wallace's death, his wife, Lady Wallace, lived alone in Hertford House until she died in 1897 – at which point the Collection was bequeathed to the nation.

And the Collection itself? Advertised as 'the finest private collection of art ever assembled by one family', if occupies the entire three floors of Hertford House. It consists of one of the world's finest collections of French paintings, porcelain and furniture along with world-famous English, Flemish and Italian paintings, drawings and watercolours. Also, you will find displays of European and Oriental armoury, ceramics, enamels, glassware, miniatures, and sculpture.

You'll find works by Gainsborough, Landseer, Turner, Rembrandt, Van Dyck, Rubens, Canaletto, Titian, Velazquez – to name just a few. Also here is Frans Hals's famous 'The Laughing Cavalier' - who is not actually laughing and apparently not a Cavalier.

Don't miss the Lower Ground Floor – one of the galleries here is the Conservation Gallery which shows some of the techniques involved in manufacturing, conserving and wearing armour – and you can try some on for yourself!

And afterwards. . . On the other side of Manchester Square (back towards Selfridges), you will find the Devonshire Arms. This cosy pub has a few collections of its own – plates, cats and. . . saucy postcards. Ooh errr. . . make mine a large one please, barmaid!

Westminster Abbey

THE HOUSE OF KINGS (AND QUEENS). . .

Westminster Abbey, Dean's Yard, London, SW1P 3PA
Telephone: 020 7222 7110
Underground: Westminster, St. James's Park
Admission: £6.00 Concessions: £3.00
Length of time required for visit: 50mins – 1 hour
Open: 9:00am – 4:45pm Mon - Fri, 9:00am – 2:45pm Sat
Web site: www.westminster-abbey.org

Directions
From Westminster
tube, take exit 5.
At street level turn
around and you'll
see the Abbey.
From St. James's
Park tube, exit on
to Tothill Street.
After a short walk
you'll soon see
the Abbey. The
main Abbey visitor
entrance is
adjacent to St.
Margaret's Church.

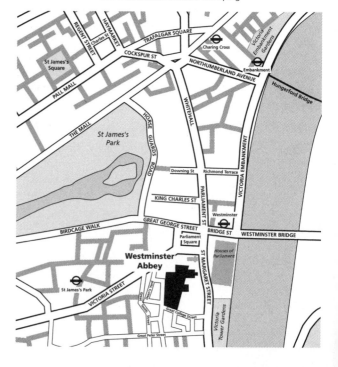

1066 was an eventful year in the history of Westminster Abbey. King Edward the Confessor had recently died and was buried in a lavish shrine in the brand new Abbey. Harold then took over as king but it wasn't long before William the Conqueror turned up, did lots of conquering, and was crowned King of England at Westminster Abbey on Christmas Day 1066.

During William's coronation the triumphant shouting in the Abbey alarmed the Norman Guards so much that they thought something had gone wrong and they started to set fire to the nearby houses. . . well, you would, wouldn't you.

So that was how coronations at Westminster Abbey began. Since then nearly all of the sovereigns of England have been crowned in the Abbey - following the precedents set by William the Conqueror (apart from the house burning). But, of course, the general public were never able to see any of this until 1953 - when Queen Elizabeth II's coronation was televised.

To make the most of your visit to the Abbey you probably ought to avoid the peak tourist periods - the queues can get lengthy. Also, we've dealt with the 'Old Monastery' section (i.e. the Chapter House, Pyx Chamber and Abbey Museum) on a separate page.

On arrival, pick up the free leaflet - this gives you a layout of the Abbey and the directions to follow for the best route through. Points of interest are clearly marked - the official guidebook gives you the same tour layout as the leaflet but the points of interest are explained in much more depth (well worth buying).

As you tour round, you'll find yourself surrounded with things from over 1,000 years of history. Elaborate shrines, statues, memorials, the actual Coronation Chair made in 1301 (complete with schoolboy carvings!) - make sure you remember to look upwards, otherwise you might miss such things as the incredible fan vaulting on the roof of Henry VII's Chapel. . .

And afterwards. . . On leaving the Abbey, cross over to Storey's Gate - the Westminster Arms can be found at number 9. Or, if you're heading back to St. James's Park tube, you will find The Sanctuary at 33 Tothill Street (near to the tube station).

Westminster Abbey: The Old Monastery

FROM THE WHORE OF BABYLON TO EERIE FUNERAL EFFIGIES. . .

Westminster Abbey, Dean's Yard, London, SW1P 3PA
Telephone: 020 7222 7110
Underground: Westminster, St. James's Park
Admission: £2.50 (Chapter House, Pyx Chamber, Abbey Museum)
Free (Cloisters, College Garden)
Concessions: £1.90 (Chapter House, Pyx Chamber, Abbey Museum)
Length of time required for visit: 50mins - 1 hour
Open: April-Oct 10:00am – 4pm Daily, Nov-March 10am-4pm (Chapter House, Pyx
Chamber, Museum) 8am – 6pm Daily (Cloisters)
10am – 4pm Tue – Thu (College Garden 10am - 6pm Apr – Sept)
Web site: www.westminster-abbey.org

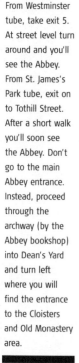

Directions
From Westminster tube, take exit 5. At street level turn around and you'll see the Abbey. From St. James's Park tube, exit on to Tothill Street. After a short walk you'll soon see the Abbey. Don't go to the main Abbey entrance. Instead, proceed through the archway (by the Abbey bookshop) into Dean's Yard and turn left where you will find the entrance to the Cloisters and Old Monastery area.

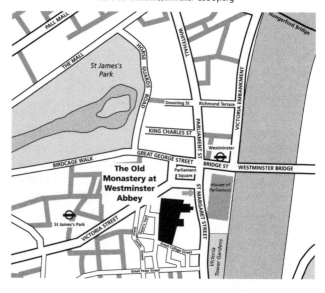

Well, it might seem a bit confusing but there are actually five attractions in one here – all within the realms of Westminster Abbey. We've dealt with the Abbey itself on a separate page. If you have an Abbey ticket, you can get reduced admission to the 'Old Monastery' sites (only £1) but to visit the whole lot in one go is a bit overwhelming if your time's limited.

So, what do we actually have here then? Firstly, the free bits. You can wander round the Cloisters, following in the footsteps of the Benedictine Monks who inhabited the medieval monastery. On Tuesdays, Wednesdays and Thursdays you can also make your way out to the secluded and tranquil College Garden – first established in the eleventh century.

Then you can buy a ticket at the Chapter House – this allows access to the Chapter House, the Pyx Chamber and the Abbey Museum. The Chapter House was built between 1245 and 1255 for Henry III – as a meeting place for the Abbey monks and the King's Great Council. Around the walls there are fascinating medieval paintings dealing with the Apocalypse – here's where you'll find the Whore of Babylon if you look closely enough.

Next door is the Pyx Chamber. It was used as a Royal Treasury for 400 years – you'll notice the massive oak doors (extra security measures were introduced after a burglary in 1503!).

Next door again you'll find the Abbey Museum in a superb vaulted room. Here you will find eerily life-like funeral effigies of several monarchs and other dignitaries – in medieval times, these effigies were placed on top of the coffin, in full regalia. The face of King Edward III, an actual death mask from 1377, really is quite spooky. . .

And afterwards. . . When you emerge from Dean's Yard, cross over to Storey's Gate – the Westminster Arms can be found at number 9. Or, if you're heading back to St. James's Park tube, you will find The Sanctuary at 33 Tothill Street.

List of Nearby Pubs

Apsley House
The Wellington Museum

Rose and Crown
2 Old Park Lane W1
Tel: 020 7499 1980
Mon-Sat 12.00-23.00, Sun 12.00-22.30

The Bank of England

Jamaica Wine House
St Michaels Alley,
Cornhill EC3V 9DS
Tel: 020 7626 9496

Simpsons Tavern
38 Ball Court EC3V 3ND
Tel: 020 76269985

The Banqueting House

The Clarence
53, Whitehall SW1
Tel: 020 7930 4808
Mon-Sat 11.00-23.00, Sun 12.00-22.30

The Old Shades
37, Whitehall SW1
Tel: 020 7321 2801
Mon 11.00-19.00, Tue-Fri 11.00-23.00,
Sat 11.00-21.00, Sun 12.00-22.30

The Barbican Art Gallery

Kings Head
49 Chiswell Street EC1Y 4SA
Tel: 020 7606 9158

The Britain at
War Experience

The Cooperage
48-50 Tooley Street SE1
Tel: 020 7403 5775

Barrowboy and Banker
6-8 Borough High Street SE1
Tel: 020 7403 5415
Mon-Fri 11.00-23.00
Closed weekends and bank holidays

The British Library

The Euston Flyer
83 Euston Road NW1
Tel: 020 7383 0856
Mon-Sat 12.00-23.00
Sat Closed between 18.00-20.00, Sun Closed

O'Neills Irish Bar
73-77 Euston Road NW1 2QS
Tel: 020 7255 9861

British Airways
London Eye

All Bar One
1 Chichley Street SE1
Tel: 020 7921 9471
Mon-Sat 11.00-23.00, Sun 12.00-10.30

Potters Bar
Travel Inn, County Hall, Belvedere Road SE1 7PB
Tel: 0870 238 3300

Jubilee Tavern
79, York Road SE1
Tel: 020 7928 7596
Mon-Fri 11.00-23.00, Sat 11.00-21.00,
Sun 12.00-16.00

The Cabinet War Rooms

Red Lion
48, Parliament Street, Whitehall SW1
Tel: 020 7930 5826
Mon-Sat 11.00-23.00, Sun 12.00-22.30

The Clink Prison Exhibition

Market Porter
9 Stoney Street, Southwark SE1
Tel: 020 7407 2495
Mon-Fri 6.30-8.30, Mon-Sat 11.30-23.00,
Sun 12.00-22.30

Design Museum

All Bar One
34 Shad Thames SE1 2YG
020 7940 9771
Mon-Fri 11.00 – 23.00, Sat 10.00 – 23.00,
Sun 10.00 – 22.30

Ask Pizza Restaurant
Spice Quay, 34 Shad Thames SE1
Tel: 020 7403 4545

Cantina Del Ponte
36c Shad Thames SE1
Tel: 020 7403 5403
12.00-15.00 Daily, 18.00-23.00 Mon-Sat

Le Pont de la Tour
36d Shad Thames SE1
Tel: 020 7403 8403
www.conran.com/eat/

The Butlers Wharf Chop House
36e Shad Thames SE1
Tel: 020 7403 3403
www.conran.com/eat/

The Dickens House Museum	**Calthorpe Arms** 252 Grays Inn Road WC1 Tel: 020 7278 4732 Mon-Sat 11.00-23.00, Sun 12.00-22.30
Michael Faraday Laboratory and Museum	**Duke of Albermarle** Stafford Street W1 Tel: 020 7355 0321 **Shelleys** 10 Stafford Street W1 Tel: 020 7493 0337 Mon-Sat 12.00-23.00, Sun 12.00-17.00
The Golden Hinde	**The Old Thameside Inn** Pickfords Wharf, Clink Street SE1 Tel: 020 7403 4243 Mon-Sat 12.00-23.00, Sun 12.00-22.30
The Guards Museum	**The Old Star** 66 Broadway SW1 Tel: 020 7222 8755
The Guildhall and Guildhall Art Gallery	**The Old Dr. Butlers Head** Masons Avenue, off Coleman Street EC2 Tel: 020 7606 3504 Mon-Fri 12.00-23.00, Closed weekends
HMS Belfast	**The Horniman at Hays** Hays Galleria, Counter Street SE1 Tel: 020 7407 1991 Mon-Sat 11.00-23.00, Sun 12.00-22.30
The Jewel Tower	**Westminster Arms** 9 Storeys Gate SW1 Tel: 020 7222 8520 Mon-Fri 11.00-23.00, Sat/Sun 11.00-18.00

Dr Johnson's House

Ye Olde Cheshire Cheese
Wine Office Court, 145, Fleet Street EC4
Tel: 020 7353 6170
Mon-Sat 11.30-23.00, Sun 12.00-15.00

The London Dungeon

Simpsons at Tooley Street
54-58 Tooley Street SE1
Tel: 020 7407 6001
Mon-Fri all day, Sat lunch only

The Monument

Hogshead
18 Fish Hill Street EC3R 6DB
Tel: 020 7929 5880

The Museum of London

The Lord Raglan
61 St-Martins-le-Grand EC1
Tel: 020 7726 4756
Mon-Fri 11.00-23.00
Closed weekends and bank holidays

The National Gallery

The Salisbury
90, St. Martins Lane WC2
Tel: 020 7836 5683
Mon-Sat 11.00-23.00, Sun 12.00-22.30

National Portrait Gallery

The Chandos
29, St. Martins Lane WC2
Tel: 020 7836 1401
Mon-Sat 11.00-23.00, Sun 12.00-22.30

Florence Nightingale Museum

Florence Nightingale
199 Westminster Bridge Road SE1
Tel: 020 7928 3027
Mon-Fri 11.00-23.00, Closed weekends

The Old Bailey

Magpie and Stump
18 Old Bailey EC4
Tel: 020 7248 5085
Mon-Fri 11.00-23.00
Closed weekends and bank holidays

The Viaduct Tavern
126, Newgate Street EC1
Tel: 020 7606 8476
Mon-Sat 11.00-23.00, Sun 12-22.30

Old Operating Theatre, Museum and Herb Garret

The George Inn
Borough High Street, Southwark SE1
Tel: 020 7407 2056
Mon-Sat 11.00-23.00, Sun 12.00-22.30

OXO Tower and Gabriel's Wharf

Doggetts
Blackfriars Bridge, Blackfriars Road SE1
Tel: 020 7633 9081
Mon-Fri 11.00-23.00, Sat 12.00-23.00,
Sun 12.00-18.00

Prince Henry's Room

Olde Cock Tavern
22 Fleet Street EC4
Tel: 020 7333 8570
Mon-Fri 11.00-23.00, Closed weekends

The Royal Academy of Arts

The Chequers Tavern
16, Duke Street SW1
Tel: 020 7930 4007
Mon-Fri 11.00-23.00, Sat 12.00-20.00,
Sun Closed

The Royal College of Surgeons of England	**The Ship Tavern** 12 Gate Street, Holborn WC2 Tel: 020 7405 1992 Mon-Fri 11.00-23.00 Closed weekends and bank holidays
Royal Opera House	**Kembles Head** 61,62 Long Acre WC2 Tel: 020 7836 4845 Mon-Sat 11.00-23.00, Sun 12.00-22.30
St Bartholomew's Hospital Museum	**The Bishops Finger** 9-10 West Smithfield EC1 Tel: 020 7248 2341 Mon-Fri 11.00-23.00 Closed weekends and bank holidays
St Paul's Cathedral	**Rising Sun** 61 Carter Lane EC4 Tel: 020 7248 4544 **Bell, Book and Candle** 42, Ludgate Hill EC4 Tel: 020 7248 1852 Mon-Fri 11.00-23.00, Sat/Sun 12.00-18.30
The Shakespeare's Globe Theatre	**The Anchor** Bankside SE1 Tel: 020 7407 1577 Mon-Sat 11.00-23.00, Sun 12.00-22.30
Sherlock Holmes Museum	**The Volunteer** 247 Baker Street NW1 Tel: 020 7486 4090 Mon-Sat 11.00-23.00, Sun 12.00-22.30

Sir John Soane's Museum

The Ship Tavern
12 Gate Street, Holborn WC2
Tel: 020 7405 1992
Mon-Fri 11.00-23.00
Closed weekends and bank holidays

Somerset House

The Coal Hole
91 The Strand WC1
Tel: 020 7379 9883
Mon-Sat 11.00-23.00, Sun 12.00-20.00
Wine bar open Mon-Sat 17.30-23.00

Art nouveau pub!
The Lyceum Tavern, 354, The Strand WC2
Tel: 020 7836 7155
Mon-Sat 11.30-23.00, Sun 12.00-22.30

Southwark Catherdral

The Mudlark
Montigue Close SE1
Tel: 020 7940 9921
Mon-Fri 11.00-23.00, Closed weekends

Tate Modern

The Founders Arms
52, Hopton Street, Bankside SE1
Tel: 020 7928 1899
Mon-Sat 11.00-23.00, Sun 12.00-22.30

The Theatre Museum

Marquess of Anglesey
39, Bow Street WC2
020 7240 3216
Mon-Sat 11.00-23.00, Sun 12.00-22.30

Tower Bridge Experience

The Anchor Tap
28 Horselydown Lane SE1
Tel: 020 7403 4637
Mon-Sat 12.00-23.00, Sun 12.00-22.30

London's Transport Museum	**The Nags Head** 10 James Street WC2 Tel: 020 7836 4678 Mon-Sat 11.00-23.00, Sun 12.00-22.30
	The White Lion 24 James Street WC2 Tel: 020 7557 9871 Mon-Thu 11.30-23.00, Fri/Sat 11.00-23.00, Sun 12.00-22.30
The Wallace Collection	**Devonshire Arms** 7 Duke Street W1 Tel: 020 7935 5887 Mon-Fri 11.00-23.00, Sat 12.00-16.00, Sun - Closed
Westminster Abbey and The Old Monastery	**The Sanctuary House Hotel** 33 Tothill Street SW1 Tel: 020 7799 4044 Mon-Sat 11.00-23.00, Sun 12.00-22.30
	Westminster Arms 9 Storeys Gate SW1 Tel: 020 7222 8520 Mon-Fri 11.00-23.00, Sat/Sun 11.00-18.00

Index – Access by Tube Station